# SAM CHOY
## Woks the Wok

# OTHER BOOKS
## by
# Chef Sam Choy

## With Sam Choy
*Cooking From The Heart*

## Sam Choy's Cooking
*Island Cuisine At Its Best*

## The Choy of Seafood
*Sam Choy's Pacific Harvest*

## Sam Choy's Kitchen
*Cooking Doesn't Get Any Easier Than This*

## Sam Choy's Poke
*Hawai'i's Soul Food*

## Sam Choy's Sampler
*Welcome to the Wonderful World of Hawai'i's Cuisine*

## Sam Choy's Cooking with Kids

# SAM CHOY
# Woks the Wok

by **Chef Sam Choy**
with **Lynn Cook**

**photography by Douglas Peebles**

edited by **Joannie Dobbs, Ph.D, C.N.S.**

MUTUAL PUBLISHING

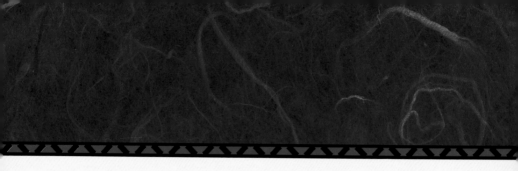

Library of Congress Catalog Card
Number: 2001093259

First Printing
1 2 3 4 5 6 7 8 9



Art direction by Jane Hopkins
    and Sistenda Yim
Food styling by Felix Lo
Design by Jane Hopkins

Softcover
ISBN 1-56647-492-2

Mutual Publishing
1215 Center Street, Suite 210
Honolulu, Hawai'i 96816
Ph: (808) 732-1709
Fax: (808) 734-4094
e-mail: mutual@lava.net
www.mutualpublishing.com

Printed in Korea

# Mahalo

A very special Mahalo to these companies whose beautiful artpieces and wares were used in all the recipe photographs. We could not have done it without you. Mahalo ā nui loa.

The Compleat Kitchen

Liberty House

Native Books & Beautiful Things

Pacific Restaurant Supply

Pier 1 Imports

Vagabond House

William Sonoma

# TABLE of Contents

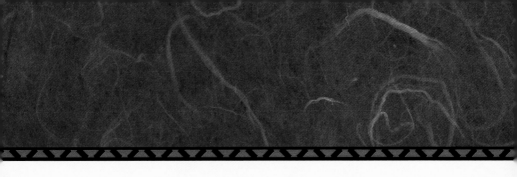

# Introduction

I love wok cooking. It is second nature to me. A wok was originally a Chinese cooking instrument. My dad was Chinese. His mom cooked over a charcoal stove. So I knew about wok cooking from a very young age. I remember that they cooked everything in a wok and left it there, or sometimes maybe put it out on a platter.

Wok cooking is not only convenient and unique, it makes what you are preparing really exciting. You know, if you are going to get a regular sauté pan and put some vegetables in it, sauté up some chicken with it, that's basically it. With a wok you have the garlic and the ginger. You let the oil smoke. That's what makes it exciting — the smell, the flavor of smoking it. That's what a wok does. It allows you to create the smoke flavor. As you stir-fry, you incorporate the flavor of the smoke into the foods.

A wok is not just a "one-pan" meal. A wok is versatile. It can be used for stir-frying, steaming, smoking, boiling, poaching, searing, simmering, braising and deep-frying. A wok offers the way to combine food flavors with the perfect cooking method. Wok cooking can be mastered by anyone. There is a flair that goes along with stirring and tossing foods in a wok. The perfect wok meal creates a sense of accomplishment as you "plate" servings. Wok cooking

enhances food color, it makes simple ingredients elegant and it can even make a "chef" of someone who can barely cook. What's more — it is fun!

Wok ingredients aren't unique. Nearly anything that you can broil, bake or saute can be cooked in a wok. It's like the times when I was in the kitchen cooking with my dad, Hung Sam Choy, and my mom, Clairemona Choy, back in the small-kid days. We would open the refrigerator. Whatever was there was dinner. Use a wok for the cooking and you can add the words "gourmet meal."

Another thing, wok cooking tends to be healthier cooking. The wok just calls out for vegetables. You stretch whatever you are cooking with vegetables. You might start out with a pound of meat but you are adding two pounds of vegetables. Basically that ratio works. You flavor it all the same. You don't need much oil. You really can't go wrong.

## TAKE A WOK

A good wok is the foundation of a kitchen. No matter how many times you are tempted into a kitchen department or cooking store, no matter how many elegant cooking utensils you purchase, once you have the wok that works for you, all the new shiny pots will begin to gather dust, like yesterday's newspaper.

Woks come in a variety of sizes and shapes. Some are deep. Some medium-deep. There is a flat bottom American-style and the rounded bottom Chinese-style that rests on a collar. I prefer the flat bottom that sits right on the stove. There are even nonstick and coated woks. Electric woks, the kind you plug in, are limited in their use. They heat up but cool down with ingredients — even quicker than a stove top wok on an electric stove. They can be useful to simmer a broth or soup and you can hold the dish on warm while you wok the main course.

About stoves: gas versus electric is a question I get asked often. It really doesn't matter. Gas heat can be better controlled. With an electric stove, what happens when you put the meat and ingredients in is that the full wok shuts down the heat, then you gotta wait until it comes back up a g a i n . With gas it is a more constant heat. If you are going to stir-fry on an electric stove, keep one big burner on high and the other on low. That way you can move it back and forth and keep the heat constant.

Another thing is the oil. Canola oil is good. With everyone watching their health, the lighter oils are best. Remember, light oil in the pan. The oil is just there to coat the pan, nothing more. With wok cooking, what you want to do is sear in the juices. You season and sear. You keep it nice and moist. Then you add the vegetables and cook al denté.

If you want fun and good eating at your parties, have two or three woks, a mountain of vegetables and some meat. You can do one shabu-shabu style. Maybe some seared ahi and a stir-fry. It is a great party idea!

The wok is really a multiethnic utensil. Adding key flavors from your (favorite) inner circle of flavors sets the mood and taste. The Chinese kitchen has ginger, garlic, soy sauce, cilantro, fermented black beans, five-spice powder, sesame seeds, hoisin sauce, and oyster sauce. If you like the Japanese Kitchen, add dashi, miso, nori, maybe some sake and wasabi or Japanese horseradish. For Indonesian, add in lemon grass, lime leaves, coconut milk, tamarind and Thai chili sauce. Indian kitchen flavors include aromatic spices and curry. For Korean, you can stir kimchee and spicy pickled cabbage. Basically a wok can take you around the world!

## THE RIGHT STUFF

Start your wok cooking equipment collection with the purchase of a flat-bottom, 14-inch carbon-steel wok with a domed lid. This wok is lightweight and conducts heat quickly. You may want some metal racks that fit into the wok for steaming. Long-handled chopsticks, a long-handled spatula-spoon combo, and a ladle are good. No need to buy more until you reach your comfort level and know the style of wok cooking where you will be using most often. Wooden steamer baskets and a rice cooker are a must. I like glass bowls for mixing sauces. A spice grinder is nice.

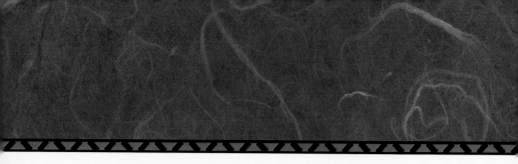

As you master the art of wok cooking and begin to build your list of "specials," you may want to add a stainless steal wok or a wok with teflon coating. There is no better way to cook a large batch of anything than a big wok. The smaller "designer" woks can be very useful for creating a sauce or side dish.

Of course you need good, sharp knives that fit your hand. Chopping boards can be wood or plastic, as long as they are kept very clean. Chopping vegetables is a major function of wok cooking. Practice on the easy ones; celery, cucumbers, onions.  You can even practice on backyard ti leaves. Once you master the larger items you can graduate to scallions, slivered fruits, nuts, seafood and meats. Chop, chop, chop until you get a fast, controlled wrist action and plates of evenly chopped veggies.

One beauty of wok cooking is that you can spread everything out. With a conventional pan, ingredients can be too done on the edge, or not cooked in the center. A wok gives the food room to be evenly cooked to perfection! Delicate ingredients don't get crushed by too much stirring. Flavors and seasonings can be more evenly distributed and blended.

Learning to wok is as easy as one, two, three.

One—shop.
Two—test.
Three—get ready, get chopped, wok!

# Wok this Way

**Poultry & Duck · Beef · Pork · Lamb · Vegetables**

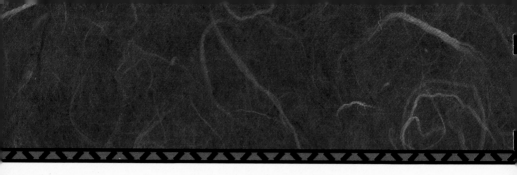

**Wok-cooked meats** are far more tender. Stir-fry, braise, deep-fry, poach, sear, stew and steam meat and vegetable combinations to create some of the best meals you can possibly serve. When you are slicing paper-thin or pounding to tenderize, you can use less expensive cuts of meat. Cost doesn't make a recipe better. It's the combination of flavors that makes the dish mouth-watering good.

One thing to remember: meat and poultry cut best when they are very cold but they need 15 to 20 minutes to come up to room temperature before you begin to cook them. Cold ingredients can cool your hot oil. Instead of being seared to seal in the juice, cold meats in hot oil will begin to steam, lose their juices and become tough, dry and tasteless. Another thing, unless the meats are marinated in a sauce, wipe them dry or dip them in flour or cornstarch. Damp ingredients and wet vegetables cause the oil to spatter and cool. Remember, don't crowd the pan. Cook smaller amounts at a time and set aside.

Slice and dice and julienne your vegetables first. Keep them refrigerated until about 15 minutes before cooking time. Once you see the beautiful color and taste the crisp-yet-cooked flavor of woked veggies, I'll bet you won't ever want to cook a vegetable in water again!

# Smoked Chicken Stir-Fry
# "It's 2 easy"

*It is two of every ingredient and too easy not to try.
Line it all up, toss it in and you'll have a dinner in two
minutes! Remember to get the oil smoking first.
The smoke is a seasoning all on its own.*

**Serves 2**

**2 tablespoons canola oil**
**2 cups smoked chicken, cut into strips**
**2 cups mixed stir-fry vegetables**
**2 teaspoons liquid dashi or chicken broth**
**2 tablespoons soy sauce**
**2 tablespoons oyster sauce**
**2 tablespoons cornstarch**
**2 tablespoons water**

Heat oil in wok until the oil begins to
smoke, then add chicken and vegetables.
Cook about 30 seconds.

Add dashi, soy sauce, and oyster sauce.
Cook about 2 minutes more until
vegetables are just tender. Mix water into
cornstarch and add to stir-fry to thicken.

Pour over rice and enjoy!

# Chicken Avocado
# and Papaya Salad

*Fresh ginger gives the wok-simmered chicken breasts
a special zing. If you have time to make your own broth, great! If not, the
low-sodium variety off the shelf works as well. My Creamy Oriental Dressing
can only be improved by the sprinkle of macadamia nuts.*

**Serves 6**

**3/4 cup Sam Choy's Creamy Oriental Dressing (see Note)**
**3 cups chicken stock or low-sodium chicken broth**
**1 thumb-size piece fresh ginger, peeled**
**3 whole, skinless boneless chicken breasts**
**2 ripe papayas, peeled, seeded and thinly sliced**
**2 ripe avocados, peeled, pitted and thinly sliced**
**Salt and pepper to taste**
**1/3 cup diced macadamia nuts**

Place 3 cups of chicken stock in a wok and add fresh ginger.
Bring the liquid to a boil and then add chicken breasts.
Simmer for 15 minutes. Remove chicken breasts from liquid
and refrigerate 1 hour.

Cut chicken into thin slices. On individual salad plates,
alternate slices of papaya, chicken and avocado. Spoon 2
tablespoons Sam's Creamy Oriental Dressing on each salad,
then sprinkle with macadamia nuts.

**Note**
**Either prepare Sam Choy's Creamy Oriental Dressing (see recipe page
126) or purchase this dressing already bottled.**

Chicken Avocado and Papaya Salad

# Sweet and Sour Chicken Tomato Stir-Fry

*The 30-minute wait while your soy-sesame mixture
soaks into the meat is worth it. This flavor is perfect for the chicken thigh.
Once you stir-fry, watch carefully so you don't overcook the chicken and make sure
you add the tomatoes last—otherwise—tomato mush!*

**Makes about 8 cups**

**2 cups Sweet and Sour Sauce (see Note)**
**I pound skinless, boneless chicken thigh**
**1-1/2 cups cornstarch**
**I tablespoon soy sauce**
**I teaspoon sesame oil**
**1-1/2 teaspoons granulated sugar**
**I clove garlic, minced**
**1/4 teaspoon fresh grated ginger**
**2 tablespoons vegetable oil**
**I medium onion, sliced into half-moons**
**I large green pepper, sliced into strips**
**2 stalks celery, thinly sliced on the diagonal**
**3 medium fresh tomatoes, cut into wedges**
**4 stalks green onions, cut into I-inch lengths**
**Salt and pepper to taste**

Rinse chicken and then slice into thin strips or bite-sized pieces. Dust chicken slices in cornstarch. Set aside.

Mix together soy sauce, sesame oil, sugar, garlic, and ginger. Massage soy-sesame mixture into meat, cover and refrigerate for 30 minutes.

Heat wok and add vegetable oil to coat sides. Add chicken and stir-fry until chicken is done but still tender. Remove chicken from wok and drain on paper towels.

Reheat wok and add onion, green pepper, and celery. Stir-fry until onions are translucent, about 3 minutes. Add Sweet and Sour Sauce to vegetables. Cook about 2 minutes, until sauce comes to a boil. Return chicken to wok, along with tomatoes and green onions, and adjust seasonings with salt and pepper if necessary.

Serve over your favorite type of rice or even fried tofu.

# Wok-Fried Curried Citrus Chicken Papaya

*Curry and fruit are a natural combo. In this dish they balance the "bite" of
the ginger, garlic and fresh cilantro. Garnish with some edible flowers.
You can find them at nearly any market. With some
fresh citrus slices, they add a bit of fun for the eye.*

**Makes about 5 cups**

**Papaya Sauce (see recipe on next page)**
**1-1/2  pounds skinless, boneless chicken thighs**
**1 cup all-purpose flour**
**2 teaspoons curry powder**
**1 teaspoon paprika**
**1 teaspoon seasoned salt**
**1 teaspoon white pepper**
**2 tablespoons canola oil**
**2 teaspoons peeled and minced fresh ginger**
**2 teaspoons minced fresh garlic**
**2 teaspoons chopped fresh cilantro**

**Garnish:**
**Papaya and citrus fruit slices**
**Cilantro sprigs**
**Edible flowers**

Rinse chicken and then slice into thin strips or bite-sized
pieces. Dust chicken slices in cornstarch. Set aside.

Mix together flour, curry powder, paprika, seasoned salt, and
white pepper and dust chicken. Set aside.

Heat wok and add vegetable oil to coat sides. Stir in ginger,
garlic, and chicken and stir-fry until chicken is done but still

recipe continued on following page

**Wok-Fried Curried Citrus Chicken Papaya**

tender. Pour Papaya Sauce over the top of the chicken and sprinkle with cilantro. Stir-fry just enough to warm sauce.

Serve chicken curry with a large scoop of rice and garnish with papaya, citrus fruit, cilantro and edible flowers.

## Papaya Sauce

**Makes about 3 cups**

1-1/2  cups orange juice
2 teaspoons curry powder
1 tablespoon cornstarch
2 cups mashed ripe papaya
1/3 cup brown sugar

Whisk together all ingredients and set aside.

# Chicken Vegetable Medley Stir-Fry

*Call this one really fast.*
*The time is in the vegetable chopping.*
*Remember, keep them the same size so they cook evenly.*
*Have everything ready and your table set. Once you stir-fry*
*the vegetables and add the chicken strips, your meal*
*is on the table three minutes later!*

**Makes about 10 cups**

**1/2 cup Teriyaki Sauce (see note)**
**1 tablespoon dark sesame oil**
**1 garlic clove, finely minced**
**1 pound skinless and boneless chicken breasts**
**2 cups broccoli florets**
**2 medium carrots, peeled and julienned**
**2 cups diced fresh or frozen green beans**
**6 rinsed and sliced mushrooms**
**1 small head bok choi, roughly chopped**

Heat 1 tablespoon oil in a wok over medium heat. Add garlic and stir. Add chicken to wok and brown 4 minutes on each side. Remove chicken and cool slightly. Slice into strips, set aside.

Prepare vegetables, then heat Teriyaki Sauce in wok over high heat. Add vegetables and stir-fry quickly until the vegetables begin to soften. Add the chicken strips, combine well and continue to cook for 2 to 3 minutes.

Serve immediately.

**Note**
**Prepare Teriyaki Sauce (see recipe page 128) or purchase this sauce already bottled.**

11

**Tri-Tip Steak & Stir-Fry**

# Tri-Tip Steak & Stir-Fry

*The longer you marinate the meat the better it is.
Overnight is best. When you pick your vegetables, think —
color. All green is dull. Add red and yellow peppers, maybe
even some orange. "Paint" your food!*

**Makes about 6 cups**

**1 pound tri-tip steak**
**1 tablespoon minced fresh garlic**
**Salt and pepper to taste**
**1 cup Sam Choy's Spicy Oriental Vinaigrette**
**1 cup Sam Choy's Wasabi Vinaigrette**
**3 cups stir-fry vegetables (your choice)**

Cut steak into thin strips. Place in a bowl
and sprinkle garlic, salt, and pepper over
steak. Add Sam Choy's Spicy Oriental
Vinaigrette and Sam Choy's Wasabi
Vinaigrette and marinate meat in the
refrigerator for a couple of hours or
overnight.

Heat wok and add steak and marinade.
Stir-fry, making sure to turn the meat back
and forth while heating. Add stir-fry
vegetables to wok and cook.

Enjoy!

# Beef Stir-Fry with Green Onions and Toasted Sesame Seeds

*The rib eye is a very flavorful cut of meat.*
*Marinating, overnight if possible, in the rice wine and sherry makes it so tender.*
*You only have to cook it just a little. Served up it looks like a picture,*
*with the toasted seeds, green onion and white rice.*

**Makes about 4 cups**

1-1/2  pound rib eye steak
1 tablespoon toasted sesame oil
1 tablespoon mirin (Japanese sweet rice wine)
1/3 cup soy sauce
2 tablespoons sherry
1 tablespoon brown sugar
2 tablespoons minced fresh garlic
2 tablespoons peeled and minced fresh ginger
1/2 round onion, thinly sliced
1 teaspoon salt
1 teaspoon black pepper

**Garnish:**
4 stalks green onion, sliced diagonally, including tops
1 tablespoon toasted sesame seeds

Cut rib eye steak across the grain of the meat into 1/4-inch slices. Then cut the slices with the grain into thin strips. Rub meat with sesame oil until it is completely absorbed.

Combine remaining ingredients in a bowl and mix well. Add meat and marinate about 30 minutes or overnight, covered, in the refrigerator.

Heat wok to high and add meat and marinade. Stir-fry quickly over high temperature.

Serve over steamed rice and garnish with green onions and toasted sesame seeds.

# Beef Noodle Salad with Peanuts

*Taste as you add in the chili, peppers, garlic and cilantro.*
*Make it full of flavor, not full of fire.*

**Makes about 6 cups**

1 pound beef round tip
6-1/2 ounces dry cellophane noodles
1 tablespoon chili oil
1 teaspoon peeled and chopped garlic
1 cup shredded snow peas
1 tablespoon seeded and sliced hot red peppers
3 tablespoons soy sauce
2 tablespoons sweet chili sauce
1/4 cup fresh chopped cilantro leaves
1/3 cup roughly chopped, roasted unsalted peanuts
1 lime, cut into 6 wedges

Slice beef into strips, first cutting across the grain and then with the grain.

Place cellophane noodles in a medium-size bowl and cover with boiling water. Allow to stand for 4 minutes or until soft; drain. Set aside.

Heat wok to high. Add chili oil and garlic and stir for 30 seconds. Add beef and stir-fry for 3 minutes or until seared. Add snow peas and hot peppers and stir-fry for 2 minutes.

Mix soy sauce and sweet chili together and add to beef mixture. Stir briefly and remove from heat.

Toss stir-fry with cellophane noodles, cilantro leaves and chopped peanuts. Place on a serving platter and serve with wedges of lime.

# Stir-Fry Pepper Beef

*For a dish with lots of flavors going on, try this. A garlic, ginger, soy and oyster sauce combo is the secret. It is the fastest of fast food. Even with the vegetable chopping you'll have dinner in less than a half hour.*

**Makes about 4 cups**

**8 ounces rib-eye beef**
**I tablespoon salad oil**
**I small onion, cut into match-size strips**
**I stalk of celery, cut into match-size strips**
**I small deseeded green bell pepper, cut into 1/2-inch strips**
**I small deseeded red bell pepper, cut into 1/2-inch strips**
**I tablespoon minced fresh garlic**
**I tablespoon peeled and minced ginger**
**1/4 cup prepared dashi or chicken stock**
**I tablespoon soy sauce**
**I tablespoon oyster sauce**
**I tablespoon cornstarch**
**I tablespoon water**
**Salt and pepper to taste**

Cut rib eye across the grain of the meat into 1/4-inch slices. Then cut the slices with the grain into thin strips. Set aside. Prepare vegetables.

Heat oil in a wok until just smoking. Stir-fry beef, onions, and celery for about 1 minute. Add bell peppers, minced garlic, ginger, dashi, soy sauce and oyster sauce. Continue to cook about 3 minutes more, being careful not to overcook the meat.

Mix water into cornstarch and stir into beef stir-fry to thicken. Add salt and pepper to taste.

Pour Pepper Beef over noodles or rice.

# Beef Sukiyaki

*This is the traditional dish and beautiful when you serve it from the wok. The key to success is keeping all your chopping as close to the same size as possible and adding them in the proper order. Add the tofu last. Be sure to turn off the heat, otherwise the tofu will break down and lose the firm texture.*

**Makes about 6 cups**

1 pound sirloin beef

1/2 cup dark soy sauce

1/2 cup mirin (Japanese sweet rice wine)

1/4 cup water

3 tablespoons granulated sugar

2 tablespoons sake (rice wine)

1 tablespoon vegetable oil

1/2 cup peeled and julienned carrot

1/2 cup julienned red bell pepper

1/2 cup Maui onion slices

1/8 cup diced green onions

4 rinsed and halved mushrooms

1/4 cup watercress

Ginger, grated to taste

4 ounces konyaku, drained and cubed (see Note)

4 ounces firm tofu, drained and cubed

Cut beef across the grain into 1/4-inch slices and then cut slices with the grain into 1 by 2-inch strips. Place in a bowl and set aside.

Mix soy sauce, mirin, water, sugar, and sake together until sugar is dissolved and then add to sliced beef. Set aside.

recipe continued on following page

**Beef Sukiyaki**

Heat wok until hot and add oil. Add stir-fry meat mixture until meat is halfway cooked. Then add carrots and peppers and stir for about 1 minute. Add remainder of vegetables and konyaku and simmer for a few minutes. Add grated ginger if desired. Turn off heat and add tofu. Let sit for about 1 minute.

Serve over rice or noodles.

**Note**
**Konyaku is also known as black bean curd and can be purchased at Asian food stores.**

**Simple Stir-Fried Beef Fajitas**

# Simple Stir-Fried Beef Fajitas

*I guess you might call this Chinese-Mex.
With the soy, cilantro, garlic and chili pepper, it has a
"wake up" taste! The hoisin sauce spread lightly
on each tortilla is the final surprise.*

**Makes 4 fajitas**

**I cup thinly sliced beef**
**2 tablespoons soy sauce**
**I teaspoon chili pepper flakes**
**I teaspoon brown sugar**
**I tablespoon peeled and minced ginger**
**I tablespoon minced garlic**
**I teaspoon fresh chopped cilantro**
**I tablespoon salad oil**
**I cup mixed vegetables (of your choice)**
**4 flour tortillas**
**4 teaspoons hoisin sauce**
**Salt and pepper to taste**

**Garnish:**
**Chopped green onions**

Marinate beef in mixture of soy sauce, chili pepper flakes, brown sugar, ginger, garlic and cilantro for about 15 minutes.

In a wok, heat 1 tablespoon salad oil. Add marinated beef and cook about 4 minutes. Add mixed vegetables and cook another 2 minutes. Add salt and pepper to taste. Remove from wok. Lightly wipe out wok with paper towel.

recipe continued on following page

Heat wok on high and heat one tortilla for about 30 seconds on each side. Remove hot tortilla and spread 1 teaspoon hoisin sauce on each one. Pour 1/4 of the beef and vegetables on each of the tortillas. Sprinkle with green onions and roll up. Repeat with other three tortillas.

Enjoy.

# Spicy Pork Tofu

**Note**
**Chinese hot bean sauce can also be called "hot bean paste."**

*A tofu lovers favorite. Season with care.*
*You want spice that lets the tofu-pork flavor take the lead.*

**Serves 4**

1 package (20 ounces) firm tofu
1 tablespoon canola oil
1 tablespoon minced fresh garlic
3/4 pound ground pork
2 to 4 teaspoons Chinese hot bean sauce to taste (see Note)
1 tablespoon soy sauce
1/4 teaspoon salt or to taste
3/4 cup water or chicken stock
1 tablespoon cornstarch plus 1-1/2 tablespoons cold water for thickening
2 stalks green onion, chopped
1-1/2 teaspoons sesame oil

Rinse tofu and drain; slice into 2-inch by 1-inch cubes. Set aside.

Heat wok or skillet, add oil, garlic, and ground pork. Stir-fry pork on high heat until done (about 2 minutes); drain off excess fat. Add hot bean sauce, soy sauce, salt, water (or chicken stock), and tofu.

Cover, bring to a boil and simmer, uncovered, for 2 minutes. Stir until any browned food is loosened. Thicken with cornstarch mixture to desired thickness. Add green onions and sesame oil. Mix gently to combine all ingredients without breaking the tofu cubes. Serve with hot rice.

# Stir-Fried Pork and Shrimp

*You have to watch the time with this flavor combo. Both pork and shrimp can be overcooked. Dice pieces to a uniform size. Line up the ingredients and have everything ready so you can spoon this directly from the pan to the plate.*

**Makes about 4 cups**

1/4 pound lean pork

1/4 pound smoked ham

1/4 pound shrimp, peeled and deveined

2 teaspoons granulated sugar

1 tablespoon hoisin sauce

2 tablespoons soy sauce

1/2 cup chicken stock or low-sodium chicken broth

2/3 tablespoons oil

1/2 teaspoon salt

1/4 cup raw peanuts

1/2 cup sliced bamboo shoots

2 sticks dried bean curd, cubed

Dice pork, ham, and shrimp if large. Set aside.

In a small bowl, combine sugar, hoisin sauce, soy sauce, and chicken stock. Mix until sugar is dissolved. Set aside.

Heat a large wok, add oil and salt. Stir-fry pork until it loses its pinkness. Add smoked ham and shrimp and stir-fry for an additional 30 seconds.

recipe continued on following page

Add peanuts, sliced bamboo shoots and bean curd. Stir-fry for an additional 1 to 2 minutes.

Stir in hoisin-chicken stock mixture and heat quickly. Cook, covered, 3 to 4 minutes over medium heat, stirring several times.

Serve immediately.

# Stir-Fried Roast Pork with Chinese Long Beans

▼▲▼▲▼▲▼▲▼▲▼▲▼▲▼▲▼▲▼▲

*You know how good those long green beans always look in the market? Well, they look even better when you stir-fry them with diced roast pork. Have the rest of your meal ready, since this takes about five minutes to prepare.*

## Makes 3 to 4 cups

1/2 pound roast pork

1/2 teaspoon brown bean sauce

1/2 clove fresh garlic, minced

10 long beans

2 teaspoons oil

1/2 teaspoon salt

1 pound long beans

1 teaspoon soy sauce

1/2 cup chicken stock

2 teaspoons cornstarch, mixed with 2 teaspoons water

Dice pork into 1/4-inch cubes and set aside.

Mash together minced garlic and brown bean sauce, set aside. Rinse and trim ends of long beans. Cut into 1-inch sections and set aside.

In a wok, heat oil, adding salt and garlic-brown bean sauce. Stir-fry diced roast pork about 1 minute, adding long beans until coated in oil. Add soy sauce, stir-frying an additional 1 minute.

recipe continued on following page

**Stir-Fried Roast Pork with Chinese Long Beans**

Stir in chicken stock and heat quickly. Cook, covered, over medium heat until beans are nearly done, about 3 to 4 minutes. Thicken with cornstarch and water mixture.

Serve immediately.

# Wok Seared Lamb

▼▲▼▲▼▲▼▲▼▲▼▲▼▲▼▲

*Make sure your slicing knife is sharp and
take care to slice the lamb thin and even. Wok the lamb after the
garlic flavors the pan. Sear it and remove. Then flavor the pan again
with the leek and onions and send that lamb right back. The
Hoisin Chili Garlic Sauce makes it all work together.*

**Makes about 4 cups**

**Hoisin Chili Garlic Sauce (see recipe on next page)**
**3/4 pound boneless lamb (leg or loin)**
**2 tablespoons rice wine or dry sherry**
**2 tablespoons soy sauce**
**2 teaspoons cornstarch**
**1/4 teaspoon black pepper**

**2-1/2  tablespoons oil, divided use**
**3 cloves fresh garlic, thinly sliced**
**1 leek, white part only, julienned**
**1/2 cup each thinly sliced red and yellow onions**
**6 green onions, julienned**

Prepare Hoisin Chili Garlic Sauce.

Cut lamb into thin slices and then into thin strips. Set aside.

Mix together rice wine, soy sauce, cornstarch, and black pepper in a bowl. Add lamb and coat. Let stand for 10 minutes.

Place wok over high heat until hot. Add 2 tablespoons of oil and coat sides. Add garlic and cook for about 10 seconds, stirring constantly. Add lamb and stir-fry for about 1-1/2  to 2

minutes until the meat is barely pink.
Remove meat from wok.

Add remaining 1/2 tablespoon oil to wok
and again coat sides. Add leek and onions
and stir-fry for 1 minute. Return lamb to
wok and add the Hoisin Chili Garlic Sauce.
Cook until lamb is heated.

Serve and enjoy.

# Hoisin Chili Garlic Sauce

**Makes 1/4 cup**

**3 tablespoons hoisin sauce**
**1 tablespoon soy sauce**
**2 teaspoons chili garlic sauce (Sambal)**

In a small bowl, mix together hoisin sauce,
soy sauce and garlic sauce.

# Pork Tofu with Maui Onion and Watercress

▼▲▼▲▼▲▼▲▼▲▼▲▼▲▼▲▼▲▼▲

*Even non-tofu lovers will enjoy this dish.
The pork combines with the seasonings, onions and watercress
to create a lovely, thick sauce. The tofu takes in the flavor
until it melts-in-the-mouth.*

**Makes about 6 cups**

**1/2 pound lean pork
1 package (20 ounces) firm tofu
1-1/2 tablespoons canola oil
1/3 cup soy sauce
2-1/2 tablespoons granulated sugar
1 finger fresh ginger, sliced
1 medium Maui onion, thinly sliced into half-moons
1/2 bunch watercress, cut into 1-inch lengths
10 green onions, cut into 1-inch lengths**

Slice pork very thin. Set aside. Cube tofu into 1-inch cubes.

Heat wok over high heat and add oil. Swirl to coat the wok. Add pork and stir until browned. Mix in soy sauce, sugar, and ginger. Stir until sauce boils, then add onion slices, watercress, and green onions. Reduce heat to medium-low and cook for 2 more minutes. Fold in cubed tofu and cook until tofu absorbs sauce.

Serve with hot rice.

**Pork Tofu with Maui Onion and Watercress**

# Stir-Fried Pork and Clams

*Never thought of combining pork and clams?*
*Try it and you'll love it. This is another instant meal that is*
*best served right from the wok. The clams go in last and are delicate.*
*Don't overcook!*

**Makes 4 servings**

**1/2 pound lean pork**
**16 small live clams (see Note)**
**1/4 cup clam juice**
**1 tablespoon cornstarch**
**2 tablespoons soy sauce**
**2 tablespoons oil**
**1/4 pound fresh mushrooms, rinsed and sliced**
**1 cup snow peas, ends removed**

Slice pork into thin strips and set aside. Rinse clams, then shell and reserve clam meat and juice.

Combine clam juice, cornstarch, and soy sauce and then add clams and toss to coat, set aside.

Heat wok and add oil. Add sliced pork and stir-fry until it loses its pinkness, about 2 minutes. Add mushrooms and snow peas, cook until softened.

Add clams and stir-fry, gradually adding in the liquid. Continue to cook until sauce is thickened, approximately 30 seconds.

Serve over rice or noodles.

**Note**
**For health safety reasons, it is important when purchasing clams that they are alive. Live shellfish will react when touched or prodded.**

# Basic Vegetable Mix

*You can make this basic vegetable stir-fry work
for a dozen different things. Pick your vegetables for their
color and for the blend of how they taste together. Experiment.
Just remember, more tender vegetables can be in
larger pieces, longer-cooking items should be sliced
very thin so they all cook at the same speed.*

**Makes 6 cups**

1 tablespoon vegetable oil
2 tablespoons butter
2 tablespoons minced fresh garlic
6 cups vegetable mix (your choice)

1 tablespoon soy sauce
1 tablespoon oyster sauce
Salt and pepper to taste

Heat wok and add oil. Add butter and garlic
and stir-fry until garlic is lightly browned.
Add vegetables and stir-fry until tender,
then soy sauce and oyster sauce. Season
with salt and pepper if necessary.

# Vegetable Stir-Fry

▼▲▼▲▼▲▼▲▼▲▼▲▼▲▼▲▼▲▼▲

*is the basic vegetable mix with the added flavor of*
*e and a bit of chicken broth. The tofu and tomato go in last*
*bey are both delicate and take very little time to cook.*

ps

u

 wedged

etable oil

 cups) mixed vegetables (your choice)

er sauce

sauce

dashi or chicken broth

 garlic sauce

h

ite or black sesame seeds

tofu and cut tomato into wedges. Set aside.

. Add mixed vegetable mix and stir-fry until
er sauce and soy sauce and stir. Pour in
auce as needed.

 liquid and mix into cornstarch. Add
re back to wok to thicken. Add tofu and
htly and cover for 2 minutes.

r fried rice and garnish with sesame seeds

# Spicy Wok-Fried Eggplant

*Eggplant and chile paste team up in the wok for an easy, popular favorite that is packed with flavor.*

**Makes about 6 cups**

2 medium Asian eggplants
2 tablespoons olive oil
1 tablespoon minced fresh garlic
2 tablespoons soy sauce
1-1/2 tablespoons brown sugar
1 tablespoon garlic chili paste
1 cup chicken stock or low-sodium chicken broth
1/8 teaspoon white pepper

**Garnish:**
5 green onion stalks, cut on bias in 1-1/2 inch-long pieces

Slice eggplants into thin diagonal slices.

Heat wok over medium heat and add olive oil, garlic, and eggplant. When garlic is lightly browned, add chicken stock and white pepper and cook for 2 to 3 minutes or until eggplant is soft but still maintains its shape.

Dissolve sugar in the soy sauce and garlic chili paste. Add to wok and cook for 2 additional minutes. Serve over rice.

# Crispy Garlic Choi Sum with Shiitake Mushrooms

*Fresh shiitake mushrooms take very little cooking. Add them to the browned garlic in the wok, add the choi sum and you'll be eating just minutes later. A splash of truffle oil dresses the dish deliciously.*

**Makes about 4 cups**

1 large head choi sum
1 cup rinsed and cleaned fresh shiitake mushrooms
1/3 cup peeled and thinly sliced garlic
1 tablespoon canola oil
Salt and black pepper to taste
1/3 cup chicken stock or low-sodium chicken broth

Wash and cut choi sum into 2-inch pieces. Slice shiitake mushrooms. Set both aside.

Heat wok and coat with canola oil, Add garlic and lightly brown. Add shiitake mushrooms and choi sum and season lightly with salt and pepper. Stir-fry for 1 minute. Add chicken stock and cook for 3 additional minutes.

To serve, spoon stir-fried choi sum and shiitake mushrooms over rice.

**Crispy Garlic Choi Sum with Shiitake Mushrooms**

# Choi Sum and Chicken with Lup Cheong

▼▲▼▲▼▲▼▲▼▲▼▲▼

*Lup Cheong lovers love this one.*
*The flavors are in harmony with the texture.*
*Pay close attention to these directions. You have to add ingredients*
*in the proper order so that each cooks perfectly.*

**Makes about 5 cups**

**I pound choi sum**
**1/2 pound skinless, boneless chicken thigh meat**
**I slice ginger, crushed**
**I clove garlic, crushed**
**I tablespoon soy sauce**
**1/4 teaspoon salt**
**1/4 pound lup cheong, sliced diagonally**
**I tablespoon salad oil**
**1/2 cup chicken broth**
**I tablespoon cornstarch for thickening**

Cut chicken into thin strips. Set aside.

Wash and drain choi sum. Separate leaves from stems and then cut stems into 3-inch pieces. Discard tough ends.

Combine chicken, ginger, garlic, soy sauce, and salt. Marinate chicken for 5 minutes.

Heat wok and lightly coat with salad oil. Add lup cheong and stir-fry for about 1 minute. Add chicken and stir-fry about 1 minute. Add choi sum stems and cook, stirring until bright green in color, about 2 minutes. Add leaves.

Mix chicken broth into cornstarch. Add cornstarch mixture to wok and cook until sauce is thickened and leaves are wilted, about 2 minutes.

# Braised Eggplant with Bacon and Tomatoes

▼▲▼▲▼▲▼▲▼▲▼▲▼▲▼▲▼▲▼▲▼▲

*This time the pan is cold when you begin
and turned down low at the end. The bacon flavor is perfect
for the eggplant and tomatoes. Make sure you stir them
gently so they keep their shape at the end.*

**Makes about 5 cups**

**2 cloves fresh garlic, minced**
**1 large round eggplant, peeled and cut in 1-inch
  cubes**
**4 medium tomatoes, peeled and quartered**
**6 bacon strips, cut into 2-inch strips**
**1/8 teaspoon salt**
**Pepper to taste**

Prepare vegetables and set aside.

Place bacon in cold wok then heat and
brown lightly (do not pour off fat). Add garlic
and stir-fry a few times.

Add eggplant cubes. Stir-fry gently to coat
with bacon fat. Reduce heat to medium and
cook, covered, until eggplant begins to
soften (about 5 minutes), stirring once or
twice.

Gently stir in tomatoes. Reduce heat to low
and cook, covered, until eggplant is done
(additional 5 minutes). Season with salt and
pepper.

# Spicy Eggplant with Chicken

*First the ginger, garlic and chili flavor the oil.*
*Then the chicken browns. Be sure to pat the eggplant dry*
*so you don't have too much liquid. Once you add the sauce you keep cooking.*
*No worry for the kids, the alcohol cooks away.*

**Makes about 5 cups**

**Prepare Soy Miso Sauce (see recipe on next page)**
**1/2 pound chicken, thinly sliced**
**5 long eggplants, cut diagonally and soaked in water**
**2 different colored bell peppers, deseeded and cut into slices**
**2 stalks green onions, cut into 1-1/2-inch lengths**
**2 white onions**
**4 tablespoons cooking oil**
**1-inch ginger, crushed**
**1 clove garlic, crushed**
**1 chili pepper, deseeded**

Slice chicken and prepare vegetables. Set aside.

Heat oil in wok and stir-fry ginger, garlic, and chili pepper for 1 minute. With a slotted spoon, remove from wok and reserve oil.

Add chicken and brown. Pat eggplant dry and add to chicken. Cook, covered, until eggplant is half done. Add bell peppers and onions. Place sauce over mixture. Cook until liquid is almost evaporated, using medium heat throughout.

Serve over rice or noodles.

# Soy Miso Sauce

**Makes 1/3 cup**

**2 tablespoons soy sauce**
**2 tablespoons miso**
**3 tablespoons brown sugar**
**1-1/2  tablespoons sake or sherry**

Mix ingredients until sugar is dissolved.

# Garlic and Island Spinach Stir-Fry

*A garlic-lover's delight. Six cloves sautéed*
*until they are crisp make a perfect balance to the wilted island spinach.*
*Be quick and don't overcook this dish!*

**Makes about 2 cups**

1 tablespoon Garlic Oil (see recipe below)
4 cups washed and torn young spinach
2 tablespoon rice or cider vinegar
Salt and white pepper to taste

Bring wok to high heat and add garlic oil. Quickly stir in spinach and season wth crispy garlic slices from Garlic Oil recipe. Stir in vinegar and add salt and white pepper.

# Garlic Oil

**Makes 1/2 cups**

1/2 cup canola oil
6 cloves of garlic, thinly sliced

In a wok, add canola oil and garlic and slowly heat. Once garlic starts frying, carefully watch it and strain out garlic once the slices are light brown and crisp. Reserve 1 tablespoon and fried garlic for above recipe. Refrigerate unused oil for flavoring other recipes.

# Wok Stew

▲▼▲▼▲▼▲▼▲▼▲▼▲▼▲▼▲▼▲▼▲▼▲▼

*Comfort food. That's what we call stew.*
*Cooked in a wok, ti becomes comfort fast-food.*
*A day later, it's even better.*

**Makes about 8 cups**

**1/2 pound boneless chuck roast, cut up into**
    **1-inch cubes**
**Salt and pepper to taste**
**Flour to dust meat (about 2 tablespoons)**
**1/4 cup celery leaves**
**1/4 cup minced onion**
**2 tablespoons salad oil**
**1 clove garlic, crushed**
**3 cups beef stock**
**1 cup chicken broth**
**6 ounces tomato paste**
**2 medium carrots, chunked**
**2 white potatoes, chunked**
**1 medium onion, chunked**
**2 stalks celery, chunked**
**2 tablespoons sweet rice flour**
**3 tablespoons water**

Sprinkle beef with salt and pepper, then
dust with flour.

Heat wok to medium and then brown meat
with garlic, minced onion, and celery
leaves. Cook for about 10 minutes on
medium or low medium, until well
browned. Keep stirring to avoid burning.

**recipe continued on following page**

Wok Stew

Add beef, chicken broth, and tomato paste. Bring to a boil and then reduce to simmer. Cover wok and cook until beef is tender, about 1 hour. Add carrots and potatoes and cook 5 minutes, then add onions and celery and cook 10 minutes more. Adjust seasoning with salt and pepper.

If the stew needs thickening, use sweet rice flour diluted with a little water. Bring the stew to a boil, add sweet rice flour mixture a little at a time, simmering and stirring until you get the right consistency. This stew is best the next day, after all the flavors have had a chance to blend.

# Wok-Fried Green Beans with Chili Garlic Sauce

*Take your time with these beans.*
*Do a few and lift them out to paper towels. Then go on*
*to the next batch. At the end they'll all be hot again with*
*a wok stir in the soy sauce, rice wine and sesame oil.*

**Makes 3 cups**

**Prepare Chili Garlic Sauce (see recipe below)**
**3 cups sliced Chinese long beans (3-inch pieces)**
**4 tablespoons canola oil**

Heat oil in wok until sizzling. Add long beans in batches, until beans are wrinkled, 3 to 4 minutes. Remove beans and drain on paper towels.

Toss beans with Chili Garlic Sauce and serve.

# Chili Garlic Sauce

**Makes 1/4 cup**

**2 tablespoons soy sauce**
**1 tablespoon minced fresh garlic**
**2 teaspoons mirin**
**2 teaspoons granulated sugar**
**2 teaspoons chili oil**
**2 teaspoons cilantro**
**Salt and black pepper to taste**

Mix all ingredients in a bowl until sugar dissolves.

Elegant Asparagus and Special Oriental Mayonnaise

# Elegant Asparagus and Special Oriental Mayonnaise

*Asparagus is an exquisite vegetable worth the time it takes to peel the stalks. This makes the spears look as precious as they taste.*

**Serves 4 to 6**

**Prepare Special Oriental Mayonnaise (see recipe on page 130)**
**1 pound fresh asparagus spears**
**1 cup rinsed enoki mushrooms**

Snap off the tough bottoms of asparagus and peel the stalks two-thirds of the way up with a swivel-bladed vegetable peeler. This makes the entire stalk tender and creates a beautiful contrast of pale and dark greens in the cooked spears.

To cook, place the spear in a wok and add water just to cover. Heat the water to boiling and cook for a few minutes until tender but still firm. Drain and pat spears dry. Serve asparagus accompanied by Special Oriental Mayonnaise.

To serve, place a small bowl of mayonnaise to one side of a large serving platter. Arrange asparagus spears in a spoke-like pattern around the bowl. Arrange small bunches of enoki mushrooms between the asparagus spokes and serve. Add oyster mushrooms as a special treat.

# Stir-Fried Wing Beans and Bamboo Shoots

*Preparing the beans for this dish is worth the time.*
*Once that is done the dish takes only minutes from wok to plate.*
*Cilantro sprinkled over perks it up just right.*

**Makes about 3 cups**

8 medium-size wing beans (also known as asparagus beans)
1 can (8 ounces) bamboo shoots
1 tablespoon canola oil
1 cup vegetable stock or low-sodium vegetable broth
1 teaspoon salt
2 teaspoons cornstarch
2 tablespoons water
1 tablespoon sesame oil

**Garnish:**
**Sprigs of cilantro**

Slice wing beans into 1-inch chunks and julienne bamboo shoots. Set aside.

In a wok, heat oil and add beans and bamboo shoots. Stir-fry for about 1 minute and add vegetable stock and salt. Heat for about 2 minutes.

In a bowl, combine cornstarch and water and stir until cornstarch dissolves. Add cornstarch to mixture and continue to cook until stock is thickened.

Remove to serving bowl and drizzle with sesame oil. Serve with white rice and garnish with cilantro sprig.

# Wok right In

**Fresh Fish · Shrimp · Crab · Scallops · Clams**

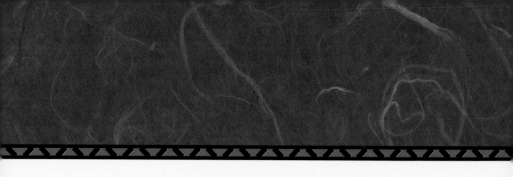

**All foods cook** quicker in a wok. This applies double to seafood. Fish and shellfish steam, sauté, deep-fry, stir-fry and sear very well. Larger cuts of fish, or even whole fish, poach perfectly in a wok. Remember, never cook fish until it flakes or shellfish until they are totally done. The heat inside keeps the seafood cooking all the way to the table.

Steaming is a favorite for fresh fish. That's where the steamer basket comes in. All the ingredients can be placed on a plate with sauces and seasoning. Then the entire dish, plate and all, is placed in a steamer. A ti leaf-wrapped fish can even go directly into the basket.

Think about how long each ingredient takes to cook. Look at the thickness and density. Layer them in the pan accordingly. Even though you are going to stir-fry, you still put things in one at a time. Make sure the first items in your wok take longest to cook. Think this through in advance. Once you start adding you can't pull back. The best you can do is move cooked items farther up on the sloping sides of the pan. Once you have the thought process mastered you can enjoy one of the best parts of wok cooking — having your friends and family around as you stir and toss their meal. Applause is always nice!

# Opah in Miso

▼▲▼▲▼▲▼▲▼▲▼▲▼▲▼▲▼▲▼▲▼▲▼

*The combination of oils and the combination of seasonings make this a most unusual fish dish. Line up all your ingredients. The cooking is fast but the eating you'll want to savor slowly.*

**Makes about 4 cups**

1/2 pound opah (moonfish) fillet (see **Note**)

1 tablespoon canola oil

1 tablespoon dark toasted sesame oil

1 teaspoon peeled and minced ginger

1 teaspoon minced fresh garlic

2 cups rinsed, trimmed, and thinly sliced fresh shiitake mushrooms

1 tablespoon mirin (Japanese sweet rice wine)

1/2 teaspoon granulated sugar

1 tablespoon miso paste dissolved in 1 tablespoon soy sauce

Salt and crushed red pepper flakes to taste

1/2 cup diced green onion stalks

1/2 cup chopped fresh cilantro

Rinse fish and cut into 3/4-inch chunks. Set aside.

Heat canola and sesame oils in wok. Add ginger, garlic, and shiitake mushrooms and stir-fry for about 1 minute. Stir in mirin and sugar; then add fish chunks and toss. Cover wok and simmer over low heat for about 5 minutes or until fish is just cooked.

Remove from heat and mix in miso-soy paste. Season with salt and crushed red pepper. Stir in green onions and cilantro and serve immediately.

**Note**
If you cannot find opah, you could substitute monchong, amberjack, jack crevalle, and trevally.

# Furikake-Kakimochi Crusted 'Ahi Steaks on a Bed of Crispy Dried Shrimp and Green Beans

▼▲▼▲▼▲▼▲▼▲▼▲▼▲▼▲▼▲▼▲▼▲▼▲▼▲▼▲▼▲▼

*Mochi crackers have a sweet-salty taste that everyone loves. Making crumbs of them, mixing with other flavors, and then searing them onto 'ahi and serving with wok-tossed dried shrimp makes an island flavor explosion in the mouth!*

**Serves 1**

**Furikake and Kakimochi Mixture (see Note)**
**6-ounce ahi steak (yellowfin tuna)**
**Wasabi paste**
**1 teaspoon canola oil**
**3 tablespoons dried shrimp**
**1 package (10 ounces) frozen French-cut green beans, thawed**
**1 teaspoon chili garlic paste**
**1 teaspoon hon dashi**

Crush Furikake and Kakimochi Mixture until crumb-like. Set aside.

Smear 'ahi steak with wasabi paste on one side and dip into Furikake-Kakimochi Mixture.

Coat wok with oil and heat until hot. Sear 'ahi until medium rare. Remove from wok.

Add dried shrimp to wok and stir until golden brown in color. Add green beans and stir for 30 seconds then add chili paste and sprinkle in hon dashi. Stir-fry for another minute and serve hot. Enjoy!

**Note**
**Furikake and Kakimochi Mixture refers to the wonderful blend of dried seaweed, bonito, and seasonings (furikake) and bite-size arare soy-flavored rice crackers. The proportions of this mixture are up to your taste preferences.**

Furikake-Kakimochi Crusted 'Ahi Steaks on a Bed of
Crispy Dried Shrimp and Green Beans

# Sam's Simple Steamed Mahimahi with Ginger and Pickled Plum

*Like the title says, Simple! Watch the steaming time.*
*Six minutes to perfect! Have the rice ready.*

**Makes 2 servings**

2 mahimahi (dolphinfish) fillets (6 ounces each)
Kosher salt and cracked white pepper to taste
8 umeboshi (pickled plums)
I tablespoon peeled and julienned ginger
I vine-ripe tomato, cut into quarters
1/2 cup picked cilantro sprigs

**Garnish:**
**Cilantro leaves**

Place about 1 cup water in wok and cover. Heat until water is producing full steam.

Meanwhile, cut mahimahi into squares and lightly salt and pepper. Place half in each of two heat-resilient ceramic bowls.

Lightly mash umeboshi between fingers and make sure to remove seeds. Divide between bowls. Then add half of julienned ginger, tomato, and cilantro sprigs.

Set bamboo steamer on top of wok and carefully place bowls in steamer and cover. Steam until fish is done (about 6 minutes for an average one-inch thick piece of mahimahi). Time will be affected by steam level and fillet thickness.

Carefully remove bowls and garnish with fresh cilantro leaves. Serve with steamed rice.

**Note**
**Other fish that can be used in this recipe if mahimahi is unavailable are drum, halibut, lingcod, orange roughy, or wahoo.**

# Smoked Fish (Wok-Style)

▼▲▼▲▼▲▼▲▼▲▼▲▼▲▼

*This swordfish dish is wonderful
whether you go to the trouble of smoking the fish or not.*

**Serves 4**

4 (5-ounce) swordfish fillets (see **Note**)

4 tablespoons room temperature unsalted
  butter

I green onion, finely sliced

1/4 teaspoon ground cumin

Salt and freshly ground black pepper to taste

4 ounces grated Monterey Jack cheese (about I
  cup)

few drops of fresh lemon juice

I tablespoon canola oil

Smoke fish if desired.

Beat butter with green onions, ground
cumin, salt and pepper to taste, cheese
and drops of lemon juice. Set aside.

Heat wok over medium-high heat and add
oil. Add swordfish fillets and cook on both
sides until well browned, about 3 minutes
on first side and 2 minutes on second side.
Turn off heat and top with onion-cheese
mixture, cover for 1 to 2 minutes. Serve
over rice or even a plate of steamed
vegetables.

**Note**
To give
swordfish a
"barbecued"
smoky flavor,
line wok with
foil and set
some hardwood
chips in wok.
Set a cake rack
2 inches above
hardwood and
set swordfish on
rack. Heat wok
and when
smoke rises,
cover fish
lightly with foil
and wok lid.
Smoke for 4
minutes.
Remove from
heat.

# Sam Choy's Garlic Ginger Salmon

▼▲▼▲▼▲▼▲▼▲▼▲▼▲▼▲▼▲▼▲▼▲

*The trick with salmon is to stop cooking before it looks done.*
*The heat in the fish keeps on cooking.*

**Makes 4 servings**

**4 salmon fillets (6 ounces each)**

**Poaching Water:**
**4 cups water**
**1/2 cup chopped cilantro**
**2 cups white wine**
**1/3 cup peeled and diced carrots**
**1/3 cup diced onions**
**1/3 cup diced celery**
**Juice of 1 lemon**
**1 teaspoon salt**
**1/2 teaspoon cracked black pepper**
**Bottled Sam Choy's Garlic Ginger Sauce**

Cut each salmon fillet into two pieces. Set aside.

In a wok, mix poaching water ingredients and bring to a boil.
Poach salmon about 3 to 4 minutes, depending on thickness
of fillets. As soon as salmon turns opaque, remove from wok.
Be careful not to overcook salmon.

To serve, generously drizzle Sam Choy's Garlic Ginger Sauce
on plate. Top with salmon fillets and again drizzle top of fish
with Sam Choy's Garlic Ginger Sauce. Serve with your favorite
vegetable and your favorite rice.

Sam Choy's Garlic Ginger Salmon

# Mahimahi Stir-Fry with Black Beans

*Create this triple-layer dish that looks beautiful and tastes better.*
*Layer the mahi with the vegetables on a large plate. Garnish. Picture perfect!*

**Serves I**

**3 pieces (about 2 ounces each) mahimahi (dolphinfish)**
**I tablespoon salad oil**
**Salt and pepper to taste**
**I tablespoon all-purpose flour**
**I cup stir-fry vegetables**
**I tablespoon minced fresh garlic**
**I tablespoon peeled and minced fresh ginger**
**2 tablespoons fermented black beans**
**I tablespoon granulated sugar**
**2 cups chicken stock or low-sodium chicken broth**
**I tablespoon cornstarch and**
**I tablespoon water for thickening**

**Garnish:**
**Curled carrots**
**Curled beets**
**Ogo**

Slice mahimahi into 2-ounce pieces. Season mahimahi with salt and pepper then dust with flour.

Heat salad oil in wok and add seasoned mahimahi. Add vegetables, garlic, ginger, black beans, sugar, and chicken stock. Cook about 2 minutes and remove fish. Continue cooking for about 3 minutes or until vegetables are just cooked. Thicken with cornstarch paste.

To serve: place 1 piece of mahimahi on plate and top with half of the vegetables. Place another piece of mahimahi on top of vegetables and add remainder of vegetables on top. Finish with the last piece of mahimahi. Pour the sauce over the top and garnish with carrots, beets, and ogo.

**Mahimahi Stir-Fry with Black Beans**

# Oven-Baked Soybean-Crusted Kalikali with Wok-Fried Vegetables

*The topping takes a bit of time for the oven-baked fish.
The vegetables take some time to chop. But 20 minutes
later you have a gourmet meal that is beautiful
and delicious. Make a show of it.*

**Serves 2**

2 kalikali fillets (any pink or ruby snapper)
Salt and pepper to taste
2 cups soybeans, ground
2 cups panko (Japanese bread crumbs)
2 ounces (1/2 stick) butter, melted
1/2 cup grated Parmesan cheese
1 tablespoon chopped fresh parsley
1 pinch of paprika
1 teaspoon minced fresh garlic
1 tablespoon chopped green onions
Wok-Fried Vegetables (see recipe on next page)

Place fillets on a lightly oiled baking pan, skin down. Season lightly with salt and pepper. In a mixing bowl, combine soybeans, panko, melted butter, grated Parmesan, parsley, paprika, garlic and green onions. Mix well. Spread mixture over fillets and bake at 350 degrees F. until browned, approximately 15 to 20 minutes.

Prepare Wok-Fried Vegetables. Serve on a large plate and place baked fish on top.

# Wok-Fried Vegetables

**Makes about 5 cups**

1 teaspoon canola oil
2 carrots, peeled and julienned
1 celery, julienned
1 red bell pepper, deseeded and julienned
1/4 cup chicken stock or low-sodium chicken broth
Salt and pepper to taste
1 bag (6 ounces) pea sprouts
1 tablespoon soy sauce
1 tablespoon sesame oil
1/2  teaspoon oyster sauce (optional)

Heat wok with canola oil and stir-fry carrots, celery, and bell pepper, tossing quickly over heat. Add chicken stock and mix. Season with salt and pepper. Top with pea sprouts, soy sauce and sesame oil. If desired, add oyster sauce.

Sam Choy's Big Aloha Fried Poke Wrap

# Sam Choy's Big Aloha Fried Poke Wrap

▼▲▼▲▼▲▼▲▼▲▼▲▼▲▼▲▼▲▼▲▼▲▼▲

*A South-of-the-Border tortilla turns multiethnic when it's folded around fried rice, beer-marinated poke and topped with my favorite dressings. You may need a double batch!*

**Makes 2 wraps**

**5 ounces poke (bite-size pieces of raw seafood)**

**Sam Choy's Big Aloha Beer to taste**

**2 ounces shredded greens (about 3/4 cup)**

**I cup fried rice (see recipe on page 118)**

**2 (12-inch) flour tortillas**

**4 tablespoons Sam Choy's Creamy Oriental Dressing (see Note)**

**4 tablespoons Wasabi Mayonnaise (see recipe on page 126)**

Marinate poke with beer to taste. Heat wok and quickly stir-fry poke. Lightly heat tortillas (one at a time) over wok. Then layer half shredded greens, fried rice, and poke onto each tortilla wrap. Top with Creamy Oriental Dressing and Wasabi Mayonnaise to taste. Roll tortilla wraps and eat!

For variations, use taro-flavored or spinach tortillas.

Note
Either prepare Sam Choy's Creamy Oriental Dressing (see recipe page 126) or purchase this dressing already bottled.

# Spicy Shrimp and Mango
# with Baby Bok Choi Salad

▼▲▼▲▼▲▼▲▼▲▼▲▼▲▼▲▼

*Crisp bok choy and seasoned shrimp make a tasteful balance.*
*Check the seasonings for your own balance.*

**Makes 4 servings**

**1 pound extra-large shrimp (16 per pound)**
**1/4 cup canola oil, divided use**
**1 red onion, sliced**
**1 tablespoon, peeled and julienned ginger**
**1-1/2 tablespoons Sambal Oelek (chili paste)**
**4 tablespoons fresh lime juice**
**2 cups diced mango, divided use for stir-fry and garnish**
**8 cups rinsed and torn baby bok choi**
**1 tablespoon Dijon mustard**
**1/8 cup rice wine vinegar**
**Salt and black pepper to taste**

Peel and devein shrimp, set aside.

In a hot wok, coat with 2 teaspoons canola oil. Add onions and ginger; stir-fry until onions become translucent. Add chili paste and shrimp and stir-fry until just cooked. Dissolve browned foods with lime juice. Add 1 cup of the diced mango and toss. Remove from wok.

In a mixing bowl, whisk together Dijon mustard, vinegar, and remaining canola oil. Check for seasoning and toss with baby bok choi. Place bok choi in the middle of the plate and surround with shrimp stir-fry. Garnish with remaining diced mango.

# Stir-Fried Chili-Garlic Shrimp

*First you add the garlic, then the shrimp,
then everything else except the bean sprouts. When you turn
the shrimp out on the crispy bed of bean sprouts and add
a little lemon and cilantro, you have flavor!*

**Makes 4 servings**

**24 extra-large shrimp (16-20 per pound)**
**1 tablespoon salad oil**
**1 tablespoon minced fresh garlic**
**1 tablespoon Sambal Oelek (chili paste)**
**1-1/2  tablespoons brown sugar**
**1/2 cup ketchup**
**1-1/2 tablespoons cider vinegar**
**2 tablespoons sherry wine**
**2 tablespoons soy sauce**
**1 bag (10 ounces) bean sprouts**
**Salt and pepper to taste**

**Garnish:**
**Chopped cilantro**
**Lemon wedges**

Shell and devein shrimp.

In a wok, heat oil. Stir-fry garlic lightly and
add shrimp. Stir-fry over high heat for 1
minute. Add remaining ingredients (except
bean sprouts) and stir-fry for about 1-1/2
minutes.

Serve on a bed of fresh bean sprouts and
garnish with chopped cilantro and lemon
wedges.

# Paniolo Prawns

*Yee Haw! These are Hawaiian cowboy prawns with a kick!*
*The simple marinade gives the prawns great flavor. Pick some favorite vegetables,*
*wok and serve them up. They won't last long!*

**Makes about 3 cups**

**1 pound fresh prawns or frozen shrimp (thaw first)**
**2 tablespoons soy sauce**
**1 tablespoon peeled and chopped ginger**
**1 tablespoon chopped fresh garlic**
**1 teaspoon chopped fresh cilantro**
**1 teaspoon brown sugar**
**1 teaspoon sesame oil**
**2 tablespoons salad oil**
**1/2 cup mixed vegetables**

**Garnish:**
**2 tablespoons green onion**

Peel and devein prawns or shrimp if necessary.

Combine soy sauce, ginger, garlic, cilantro, brown sugar, and sesame oil until sugar is dissolved. Then marinate fresh prawns or thawed shrimp about 15 minutes or up to 1 hour in the refrigerator.

Heat salad oil in wok, add shrimp and cook about 3 minutes. Stir-fry in mixed vegetables and cook for another 3 to 5 minutes.

# Kahuku Speared Prawns

*These guys don't lose their heads (or tails)!*
*Take the time to spear the prawn with the carrot and broccoli.*
*They cook so quickly and look so nice resting on the*
*mushroom cap. This is a real dress-up dish for your dinner.*

## Makes 5 servings

**2 pounds large prawns (10 per pound)**

**1/2 pound broccoli florets with stalk attached**

**1 carrot, cut into 20 strips about 2-1/2 inches in length**

**1 cup chicken stock or low-sodium chicken broth**

**1 tablespoon soy sauce**

**1 tablespoon sherry**

**1 teaspoon peeled and minced ginger**

**1 teaspoon minced fresh garlic**

**1 tablespoon cornstarch**

**2 tablespoons canola oil**

**20 fresh shiitake mushrooms, rinsed**

Peel shell from tail of prawns, leaving head and tail attached; devein. Make two slits in the back of each prawn for spearing with broccoli and carrots. Spear each prawn with a broccoli floret stalk and a carrot strip.

Combine chicken stock, soy sauce, sherry, ginger, garlic and cornstarch; blend well.

Heat canola oil in a wok and gently stir-fry prawns, about 2 minutes. Remove prawns from wok.

recipe continued on following page

**Kahuku Speared Prawns**

Add stock mixture to wok and bring to a boil. Reduce heat and simmer, stirring frequently, until thickened. Add prawns and shiitake mushrooms; cook 1 minute.

To serve, place each prawn on top of mushroom cap.

# Sam's Shrimp Stir-Fry

*It is done so fast it's hard to believe.*
*Shrimp can be easily overcooked so watch the time. Set them aside*
*while you do the vegetables, then let them have only one more minute in the wok!*

**Makes about 8 cups**

I pound shrimp, peeled and deveined
2 tablespoons vegetable oil, divided use
I tablespoon peeled and minced ginger
2 whole green onions, trimmed and sliced
2 teaspoons minced fresh garlic
4 cups broccoli florets, separate small florets
I can (15 ounces) baby corn, drained
1/2 cup chicken stock or low-sodium chicken broth
2 tablespoons rice wine (see Note)
2 tablespoons soy sauce
Salt and pepper to taste
I tablespoon sesame oil

Heat wok to a moderately high heat and add 1 tablespoon oil. Add shrimp and stir-fry until shrimp turn pink (about 2 minutes) Transfer shrimp to a plate.

Add remaining oil to wok and add ginger, green onions, and garlic; stir-fry for about 30 seconds. Add broccoli and baby corn to wok and stir-fry for 1 minute; then add chicken stock, rice wine, soy sauce, and salt and pepper to taste. Cover and steam 2 minutes.

Return shrimp to wok and stir-fry until heated through (about 1 more minute). Drizzle sesame oil over shrimp and vegetables and toss lightly. Serve.

**Note**
**Sherry can be used in place of rice wine.**

# Wok-Flashed Salt and Pepper Shrimp with Sam Choy's Island Lup Cheong Fried Rice

*Shrimp keep their coats on. That's leaving the shell on, tossing them with the peppercorns and giving them a quick fry before they get comfortable on a bed of my Island Fried Rice.*

## Makes 4 servings

Sam Choy's Island Lup Cheong Fried Rice  (see recipe on page 118)
1-1/2 pounds extra-large shrimp (16 per pound)
1/2 tablespoon ground black peppercorns
1 teaspoon ground white peppercorns
1/2 teaspoon ground Szechwan peppercorns
1 tablespoon kosher salt
1/2 cup cornstarch
1/4 cup canola oil
4 stalks green onions, minced

Peel and devein shrimp. Soak shrimp in salty cold water for about 20 minutes and rinse thoroughly. Set aside.

Mix peppercorns, kosher salt, and cornstarch in a large bowl and dredge shrimp. Set aside.

Add oil to a very hot wok and stir-fry shrimp quickly. Stir in green onions and cook until shrimp are pink.

Serve with Sam Choy's Island Lup Cheong Fried Rice.

# Spicy Shrimp Broccoli

*Peeling shrimp takes some time, but fresh shrimp are worth it.*
*Blanch the broccoli ahead and have everything ready, including the rice or noodles.*
*Cooking this dish is counted in seconds.*

**Makes about 5 cups**

1 pound large shrimp (21 to 25 per pound)
1-inch piece ginger, peeled and minced
2 cloves garlic, minced
2 green onions, thinly sliced
3/4 cup chicken stock or low-sodium chicken broth
1/4 cup soy sauce
2 tablespoons dry sherry
1 teaspoon sesame oil
1 tablespoon granulated sugar
1 tablespoon cornstarch
1/4 teaspoon black pepper
1/8 teaspoon crushed red pepper flakes
3 tablespoons canola oil
1 pound blanched broccoli florets (see Note)

Peel and devein shrimp. Set aside.

Combine ginger, garlic and green onions; set aside.

Combine chicken stock, soy sauce, sherry, sesame oil, sugar, cornstarch, black pepper and crushed red pepper flakes; blend well until sugar is dissolved.

In a wok, heat 2 tablespoons of canola oil over medium-high heat. Stir-fry ginger mixture for 15 seconds, add shrimp and cook, stirring constantly for 1-1/2 minutes. Add the remaining

recipe continued on following page

**Spicy Shrimp Broccoli**

1 tablespoon oil and broccoli; stir-fry for 30 seconds. Stir in stock mixture and cook, stirring constantly until mixture thickens, about 1 minute.

Serve over rice or noodles.

**Note**
**Broccoli can be blanched in boiling water or a microwave. In a glass container with a glass lid, place broccoli and add a few tablespoons of water. Microwave on high setting for 1 to 2 minutes.**

# Creamy Portuguese Grits with Stir-Fried Shrimp

*You might say this is "Southern cookin'" island style. Cream, cheese, butter, sausage and creamy grits make a delicious bed for simple stir-fried shrimp.*

**Makes 4 servings**

**2 quarts chicken stock or low-sodium chicken broth**

**8 ounces grits**

**3/4 pound extra-large shrimp (16 to 20 per pound), peeled and deveined**

**Salt and pepper to taste**

**1 tablespoon minced fresh garlic**

**1 tablespoon soy sauce**

**3 tablespoons all-purpose flour**

**1 tablespoon oil, divided used**

**1 tablespoon butter**

**1 whole onion, diced**

**6 ounces Portuguese sausage, diced**

**3 tablespoons diced green onions**

**1 cup heavy cream**

**5 ounces diced Provolone cheese (about 1 cup)**

Bring a pot of chicken stock to a boil and gradually stir in grits until a thick but smooth consistency is reached. Lower heat.

Prepare shrimp by seasoning with salt, pepper, garlic and soy sauce. Coat with flour. Coat wok with 2 teaspoons oil and heat and quickly stir-fry until shrimp turns pink. Remove from wok.

**recipe continued on following page**

Reheat wok and add remaining oil, butter, and onions. Add Portuguese sausage and green onions. Spoon cooked grits from pot and add to sausage mixture. Pour in heavy cream and Provolone cheese. Stir together.

Serve shrimp over Portuguese grits.

# Wok-Stirred Scallops and Rice Stick Noodles in Black Bean Sauce

*The delicate scallop and the black bean and pepper combo make the perfect couple. Taste to fit your "heat" quotient.*

**Makes 4 servings**

8 ounces rice stick noodle

2 Hawaiian chili peppers

1-1/2 pounds scallops

2 teaspoons canola oil

1 tablespoon minced fresh garlic

1 tablespoon peeled and minced ginger

2 teaspoons crushed fermented Chinese black beans

1/2 cup white wine

2 diced Roma tomatoes

1 tablespoon fish sauce

2 cups chicken stock or low-sodium chicken broth

1 cup fresh Thai basil, chopped

1 bunch chives, minced

Salt and white pepper to taste

**Garnish:**
lime, quartered

Place rice sticks in large bowl and cover with boiling water; let stand until tender to the bite (about 30 minutes); drain well and set aside.

recipe continued on following page

Carefully mince chili peppers and set aside. Thoroughly wash hands after touching peppers.

Coat a very hot wok with oil, add scallops, garlic, ginger, chili peppers, and black beans. Stir quickly for 5 minutes. Dissolve food particles with white wine and simmer until liquid volume is reduced by 50 percent.

Add tomatoes, fish sauce, chicken stock and noodles, combine well. Add basil, chives, and butter. Check for seasoning.

Serve with lime quarters to be squeezed on scallops right before eating.

# Clams with Sam's Black Bean Lup Cheong Sauce

*Black beans are really taking off.*
*At first it was just an island flavor, now it has gone "mainstream."*
*With the delicate flavor and texture of clams, this jazzy*
*sauce is a perfect balance.*

**Makes 2 servings**

1 dozen Manila clams
1/3 cup salt (for cleaning clams)
1 gallon water
1 tablespoon salted black beans
3 ounces lup cheong (Chinese pork sausage)
1 teaspoon peanut oil
1/4 cup butter
1 tablespoon peeled and minced ginger
2 teaspoons minced fresh garlic
1/4 cup minced cilantro (Chinese parsley)
1/4 cup minced green onions
1/4 to 1/2 teaspoon minced Hawaiian chili peppers
1 cup chicken broth
1 tablespoon oyster sauce
2 tablespoons soy sauce
1 tablespoon sugar
3 tablespoons cornstarch
3 tablespoons water

Clean clams (see Note).

Soak black beans in water for 20 minutes; rinse, drain, and mash.

Slice lup cheong into thin strips.

In a wok, heat peanut oil and lup cheong and stir-fry for 3 minutes, Add butter, ginger, garlic, black beans, cilantro, green onions, and Hawaiian chili peppers; stir-fry for a few minutes. Add chicken broth and bring to a boil. Add clams and stir well to blend with flavors. Cover wok and boil until clams open (about 2 to 3 minutes).

Remove clams and place in a colander nestled in a bowl. Set clams aside and return drained juices to wok along with oyster sauce, soy sauce, and sugar. Stir well and bring liquid to a boil for about 30 seconds.

Mix cornstarch with water to form a paste and stir into wok liquid. Heat and stir until liquid thickens. Return clams to wok and toss to coat.

Note
**Place clams in solution of 1/3 cup salt in 1 gallon of cold water. Let stand for 15 minutes. Rinse clams and repeat again. Thoroughly scrub shells with a brush.**

# Stir-Fried Abalone
# with Chicken and Asparagus

*Abalone is an island favorite. Keep things in order here,*
*chicken first, then the abalone, and then the asparagus. All three cook quickly.*
*The wok brings this medley of flavors into perfect harmony.*

**Makes about 7 cups**

1 can (15-ounces) abalone
1 small skinless, boneless chicken breast
2 pounds fresh young asparagus
1 cup abalone liquid
1 cup chicken stock or low-sodium chicken broth
1 tablespoon sherry
1/2 teaspoon granulated sugar
1/2 teaspoon salt
2 tablespoons oil
1/2 cup sliced bamboo shoots
1 tablespoon cornstarch and
2 tablespoons water for thickening

Drain liquid from canned abalone, and reserve liquid for later use.

Cut both abalone and chicken into 1-inch cubes and set aside separately. Then snap off and discard the tough bottoms of asparagus and cut asparagus into 1-inch diagonal sections. Set aside.

Combine abalone liquid, chicken stock, sherry, sugar and salt in a bowl, set aside.

Heat wok, add oil and stir-fry chicken cubes until cooked. Add abalone and bamboo shoots, cooking only to heat, about

1 minute. Add asparagus sections and then chicken stock and sherry mixture. Bring to a boil, stirring gently.

Mix cornstarch and water into a paste and stir into stock until thickened.

Serve at once.

# Spicy Lemon Thai Soup
# with Mussels and Leeks

*If you love mussels, you won't want
to miss out on tasting this — it's unbelievable!*

**Makes 4 servings**

I pound mussels
I to 2 fresh Hawaiian chili peppers
2 tablespoons canola oil, divided use
I cup sliced onions
I thumb of ginger, sliced
1/4 cup sliced lemon grass stalks, white part only
4 to 6 kaffir lime leaves
2 tablespoons fish sauce
8 cups chicken stock or low-sodium chicken broth
I large carrot
2 large leeks, julienne white part only
Salt and white pepper to taste

Prepare mussels (see Note). Set aside.

Remove the stem from the chili pepper and slice. Be careful
to wash hands thoroughly after touching these peppers
because they are very hot. Set aside.

Coat wok with 1 tablespoon oil and heat. Add onions and stir-
fry until caramelized (browned). Add ginger, chilies, lemon
grass and kaffir lime leaves. Add fish sauce and dissolve
browned particles from side of wok.

Add chicken stock, stir, and slowly simmer until stock is
reduced by about 25 percent. Strain soap and add salt and

recipe continued on following page

**Spicy Lemon Thai Soup with Mussels and Leeks**

pepper if necessary. Pour soup into a container with a lid and keep hot until served.

While soup is simmering, use a swivel peeler to remove outside layer of carrot and discard. Then peel carrots producing thin carrot spaghetti for topping. Set aside.

Add remaining oil and reheat wok to high. Stir-fry mussels until they start to open. Add julienned leeks and carrots, and season. Stir and check again for flavor. Serve immediately.

**Note**
**It is important to make sure your mussels come from a safe source. Then, mussels taken from the wild need to be cleaned by scrubbing them under cold water with a stiff brush. And to remove sand, drop them in salted water for a short time. Cultivated mussels generally come ready to cook.**

# Stir-Fried Lobster and Mixed Vegetables

▼△▼△▼△▼△▼△▼△▼△▼△▼△▼△▼

*Introduce bamboo shoots and button mushrooms*
*to the "King of Seafood" and the result is a quick, light and elegant*
*dish that will certainly impress your family and friends.*

**Makes about 4 cups**

I pound lobster meat
2 tablespoons peeled and minced ginger
1/2 cup chicken stock or low-sodium chicken broth
2 tablespoons sherry
1/2 teaspoon granulated sugar
3 tablespoons canola oil
1/2 teaspoon salt
I garlic clove, crushed
1/2 cup sliced (1/4 inch) celery
1/2 cup cubed (3/4 inch) bamboo shoots
I small cup rinsed button mushrooms
I tablespoon cornstarch
2 teaspoons soy sauce
2 tablespoons water
few drops of sesame oil

**Garnish:**
1/4 cup blanched and toasted almonds

Cut lobster meat into 1/2-inch cubes.

Combine ginger with chicken stock, sherry and sugar and stir until sugar is dissolved. Set aside.

In a wok, heat oil, adding salt and garlic. Add lobster and stir-fry for 1 minute. Add vegetables and cook for an additional 2 minutes.

Stir in ginger stock mixture, heating quickly
for 3 minutes on medium heat. Blend
cornstarch, soy sauce, and cold water into
a paste, stirring into liquid to thicken.

Sprinkle with sesame oil and finish with a
garnish of toasted almonds.

# Crab Bienet

▼▲▼▲▼▲▼▲▼▲▼▲▼▲▼▲▼▲▼▲▼▲

*A bienet is New Orleans walk-around food.*
*Deep-frying should be for a special meal, not for every day,*
*but with the crab inside this one you may find lots of reasons for a "special meal!"*

**Makes about 6 cups**

**I pound crab meat**

**I tablespoon canola oil**

**1/2 cup chopped onion**

**1/2 cup chopped celery**

**1-1/2 cups flour**

**I teaspoon baking powder**

**3 eggs, beaten**

**Salt and pepper to taste**

**Canola oil for frying**

**Optional Garnish:**

**I tablespoon Parmesan cheese**

**Tabasco to taste**

Tear crab meat into large pieces and set aside.

Heat wok to medium and coat with oil. Add onion and celery and stir until onion has become translucent and caramelized. Remove from wok and set aside. Wipe inside of wok with paper towel.

In a large bowl, combine flour and baking powder and hen mix in eggs. This makes the batter needed for the recipe. Mix in crab meat and season with salt and pepper. Add onions and celery and mix until evenly combined.

Add about 2 inches oil to bottom of wok and heat until sizzling. Spoon large pieces of crab mixture into heated oil.

Deep-fry until golden brown and drain on paper towel. Repeat with remaining crab mixture.

Add a sprinkle of Parmesan cheese or a drop of Tabasco if desired.

# Gingered Crab

▼▲▼▲▼▲▼▲▼▲▼▲▼▲▼▲▼▲▼

*Crab and ginger. Easy and quick to make.*
*If you use crab meat, you have "cleaner" fingers, but not as much fun.*
*The sauce poured over is even better when you can lick your fingers!*

**Serves 4**

**3-pounds whole Dungeness crab (see Note)**
**3 tablespoons vegetable oil**
**1/2 cup peeled and julienned ginger**
**2 cups chicken stock or low-sodium chicken broth, divided use**
**1-1/2 tablespoons water**
**4 green onions, julienned**

To clean a crab, hold the legs down with the right hand while gripping the head of the crab from underneath with the left hand. With even pressure, pull the "helmet" off the crab. Remove gills and mouth. Using a wooden mallet, crack the claws into serving-size pieces. Leave the body intact.

Heat vegetable oil in wok and stir-fry crab and 1/4 cup of ginger for 1 minute. Add 1 cup of the chicken stock, cover and steam for 5 minutes. Remove crab to a heated serving platter.

Add the remaining cup of chicken stock and bring to a boil. Blend cornstarch and water to make a smooth paste. Stir cornstarch mixture into chicken stock. Reduce heat and simmer, stirring frequently, until thickened. Stir in the remaining 1/4 cup ginger and green onions. Pour over crab and serve immediately.

Serve with white or brown rice.

**Note**
**You can make this wonderful flavored dish even quicker by substituting 1 to 1-1/2 pounds of crab meat for whole Dungeness crab.**

# Chili Clams

▼▲▼▲▼▲▼▲▼▲▼▲▼▲▼▲▼▲▼▲▼▲▼▲▼

*The chili sauce makes this dish. It is quick and easy.*
*Soaking and steaming the clams takes a bit of time. But it is all worth it*
*when you take your first bite!*

**Makes 4 servings**

**Prepare Chili Sauce (see recipe on next page)**
**2 pounds Manila clams (see Note)**
**1/2 cup water**
**1-1/2 tablespoons oil**
**1-1/2 teaspoons peeled and minced ginger**
**1-1/2 teaspoons minced fresh garlic**
**1/2 cup minced onion**
**1/2 pound tomato, cut into 1/4-inch pieces**
**1/8 teaspoon salt**
**3 green onions, cut into 1/4-inch pieces diagonally**

Place the clams in a wok, add water and bring to a boil over high heat. Once the clams begin to open, transfer to a bowl until all of the clams have opened. Discard any clam that does not open and discard the liquid from the pot. Save the clams and their liquid in the bowl.

Reheat wok over high heat and add oil, coating sides. Add ginger and garlic and cook for 30 seconds. Add the onion and cook for another minute. Lower the heat and continue cooking for another 5 minutes, stirring occasionally.

Add tomato and salt; increase heat to high and stir well. Lower heat and cook until the tomato and onion reach the consistency of purée. At this time bring mixture to a boil. Add clams and liquid and stir well and continue to cook for 2 minutes. Add green onions and serve with hot rice.

# Chili Sauce

**Makes about 1/4 cup**

**4 teaspoons chili sauce**

**1 tablespoon soy sauce**

**1-1/2 teaspoons white rice vinegar or distilled vinegar**

**2 tablespoons dry sherry**

**1/4 teaspoon salt**

**1 tablespoon granulated sugar**

**Pinch freshly ground pepper**

Combine the chili sauce ingredients in a bowl and set aside.

# Stir-Fried Dungeness Crab and Black Beans

*You need big napkins for this one.*
*The crab in the shell is infused with the thick sauce flavored*
*by fermented black bean paste. It is perfect on any*
*variety of stir-fried vegetables. Dig in!*

**Makes about 4 cups**

1 whole Dungeness crab (about 1 pound crab meat)
2 tablespoons vegetable oil
2 tablespoons fermented black bean paste
1 cup chicken stock or low-sodium chicken broth
1 tablespoon soy sauce
1 tablespoon oyster sauce
1 teaspoon sesame oil
1/4 teaspoon chili flakes
1 tablespoon granulated sugar
1-1/2 tablespoons cornstarch
3 tablespoons water
2 cups Vegetable Stir-Fry (see recipe on page 38)

Rinse crab, remove the top shell. Separate the claws from the body, discarding head and innards. Crack the claws with pallet or pliers, and quarter the body.

In a wok, heat oil and then add crab and black bean paste. Stir for about 2 minutes.

Mix together chicken stock, soy sauce, oyster sauce, sesame oil, chili flakes, and sugar and add to wok. Cook for 5 minutes. Mix cornstarch and water and add to wok to thicken sauce.

Serve with cooked Vegetable Stir-Fry.

# Chef Sam's
# Wok-Seared Scallops

*Ginger, garlic and scallops are a perfect marriage of flavors.
Tasting the pureness of the scallop is the important thing.
Not overcooking is even more important. Think delicate!*

**Makes about 2 cups**

3/4 pound fresh scallops (see **Note**)
2 teaspoons cornstarch
1/2 teaspoon salt

**Sauce:**
1/4 cup tomato sauce
1/4 cup rice wine or dry sherry
2 teaspoons chili garlic sauce (Sambal)
2 teaspoons oyster sauce
1-1/2 teaspoons granulated sugar

2 tablespoons oil, divided use
1 teaspoon minced fresh garlic
1 teaspoon peeled and minced ginger

Pat scallops dry with paper towels and
place in a small bowl with cornstarch and
salt. Let stand for 5 minutes.

Meanwhile, combine tomato sauce, rice
wine, chili garlic sauce, and sugar and mix
until sugar is dissolved. Set aside.

Coat wok with 1 tablespoon of oil and heat
over high heat. Add garlic and ginger and
cook for about 10 seconds, stirring

recipe continued on following page

103

constantly. Add tomato sauce mixture and simmer over medium heat for 2 to 3 minutes. Remove from heat and keep warm.

In a second wok, add remaining oil and heat over medium-high until hot. Add 1 tablespoon of oil, coating the sides. Add scallops and cook until they turn opaque in color. This takes about 2 minutes on each side. Pour sauce on a serving plate and arrange scallops over the sauce.

Wonderful as is or better when served with your favorite vegetable.

**Note**
**Scallops are quite perishable. Fresh scallops should have a sweet, mild odor and feel slightly springy. Once purchased, refrigerate them in a plastic bag over a bowl of ice.**

Chef Sam's Wok-Seared Scallops

# Stir-Fried Tofu and Scallops with Mixed Greens

▼▲▼▲▼▲▼▲▼▲▼▲▼▲▼▲▼▲

*Here is what I call an "Asian-Island" flavor.*
*The tofu, scallops and mushrooms have similar texture,*
*blending so well with the pepper, garlic and ginger. Remember to*
*turn off the heat before adding the long rice.*

**Makes about 6 cups**

1 package (2 ounces) long rice
1 package deep fried tofu
8 ounces fresh scallops (see Note)
6 fresh shiitake mushrooms, rinsed
2 tablespoons oil
4 cups mixed vegetables
1 tablespoon sake
1 tablespoon minced fresh garlic
1 tablespoon peeled and grated ginger
1 teaspoon hot pepper flakes
1/2 teaspoon salt
1 teaspoon ground white pepper
2 tablespoons soy sauce

Soak long rice in hot water for 10 to 15 minutes. Drain.

Cube the tofu into bite-size pieces; cut scallops and shiitake mushrooms into 1/4-inch slices. Set aside separately.

Heat well-oiled wok over medium heat. Add scallops and shiitake mushrooms and stir 30 seconds. Add mixed vegetables, sake, garlic, ginger, hot pepper flakes, salt and

pepper and stir another 30 seconds.
Finally stir in soy sauce and tofu and cook
until vegetables are tender.

Seafood Pinacbet

# Seafood Pinacbet

▼▲▼▲▼▲▼▲▼▲▼▲▼▲▼

*Surround your wok with the dishes of chopped veggies and
seafood. Have fun as you add dish after dish!*

**Makes 3 servings**

**4 ounces lean pork**
**2 tablespoons chopped fresh garlic**
**2 tablespoons peeled and chopped ginger**
**2 ounces 'opae (dried shrimp)**
**2 tablespoons soy sauce**
**I round onion, thinly sliced**
**I tomato, quartered**
**3 cups chicken stock or low-sodium chicken
  broth**
**Salt and pepper to taste**
**I/4 cup fish sauce**
**3 eggplants, thinly sliced**
**3 bitter melons, thinly sliced**
**8 fingers okra, sliced**
**I cup diced long beans**
**I/4 pound crab meat**
**4 ounces fresh fish fillet**
**9 mussels (see note on page 92)**
**6 scallops (see note on page 107)**
**6 shrimp, peeled and deveined**

Cut pork into bite-size pieces and prepare
all vegetables and seafood. Set aside
separately.

In a large, lightly oiled wok, heat pork and
add garlic, ginger and dried shrimp. Mix
together, then drizzle with soy sauce and

recipe continued on following page

stir again. Add onion and tomato and chicken stock and bring to a boil, stirring occasionally. Season with salt and pepper.

Add fish sauce and mix in eggplant, bitter melon, okra and long beans. Stir and let mixture sit a few minutes.

Add seafood and cook until stew is ready.

# Wok it on Home

## Rice • Noodles • Sauces

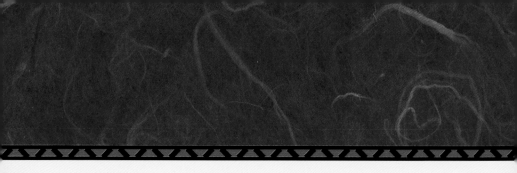

**If you think** of stir-fry as oily rice dishes or limp, drowning vegetables, you haven't had good stir-fry. If you think of noodles as a heavy, cold-weather meal, you haven't had good Asian noodle dishes. Rice and noodles can be cooked ahead and then mixed into the stir-fry. They can be simmered right in the wok in a light broth for a big rice main dish or a light noodle soup. The wok and rice were made for each other—island fast food of the best kind.

Remember, you use just a tiny bit of oil because you will be tossing the rice or noodle over and over with your spatula. The same rice dish can be Asian, Indonesian, Thai or any other nationality by just a simple change in seasoning. This is where you can open the refrigerator and add nearly anything to the noodle or rice mixture. Raisins, nuts, chopped onion, even corn cut off the cob. It all adds color and flavor so you eat "pretty," as well as delicious.

With a wok and some hot oil you can make the fluffy, exploded Thai noodles, noodle nest baskets for seafood, and even the island "comfort food," fried saimin. Noodles are light and can be easily overcooked. Add them last if you have pre-cooked them in broth or seasoned boiling water. In China they say noodles bring long life and good luck.

Good luck is easy to come by when you are making sauces in a wok. Flavored oils, Chef Sam Choy bottled sauces, spiced vinaigrettes can all be used to create the perfect finishing sauce for your entrée masterpiece. Dressings and sauces are easy to prepare in advance. Small bowls of a variety of flavors are great for dipping or adding to the main dish right at the table. Experiment! Take a chance on flavors.

# Basic White or Brown Rice

▼▲▼▲▼▲▼▲▼▲▼▲▼▲▼▲▼▲

*Rice. It's that "staff of life" thing.*
*Rice belongs with nearly every meal. If you don't have*
*a rice cooker, it is still easy to fix. You have choices in rice*
*size, type and even flavor. You can even use stock or a*
*flavor cube to change the taste of a pot of rice.*
*Experiment. Have some fun!*

## Rice Cooker Method

**Approximate Yield: 3 cups**

**White Long-Grain Rice: 1 cup rice to 1 cup water**

**White Medium-Grain Rice: 1 cup rice to 1 cup water**

**Brown Rice: 1 cup rice to 2 cups water**

1. Combine rice and water. Cover and press "Cook" button. Cooking will take 30 to 40 minutes.
2. When cooked, fluff rice, cover and allow to sit for 5 minutes before serving.

## Stove-top Method

**Approximate Yield: 3 cups**

**White Long-Grain Rice: 1 cup rice to 1-1/4 cups water**

**White Medium-Grain Rice: 1 cup rice to 1-1/2 cups water**

**Brown Rice: 1 cup rice to 2-1/4 cups water**

1. In a 2-quart saucepan, bring water (and salt if added) to a boil. Add rice. Over a

very low heat, cover and cook until water is absorbed
(about 15 minutes).
2. Remove from heat and stir once. Replace cover and let
stand for 5 to 10 minutes before serving.

## Microwave Method

**Approximate Yield: 3 cups**
**White Long-Grain Rice: 1 cup rice to 1-3/4 to 2 cups water**
**White Medium-Grain Rice: 1 cup rice to 1-1/2 to 1-3/4 cups water**
**Brown Rice: 1 cup rice to 2-1/2 cups water**

1. Add rice to a 1-1/2 quart glass casserole dish, cover.
2. Heat on high for 5 minutes; medium for 15 minutes.
3. Remove from microwave and let sit 5 minutes (with cover
on) before serving.

# Sticky Rice

*This is what you find beside the yummy Thai food
when you eat out. Make it at home in the wok and it will taste
even better. The overnight soaking is what makes it best.*

**Makes about 4 cups**

**2 cups sticky rice**
**Water**

**Equipment needed:**
**Wok with domed lid**
**Rack that fits inside wok (like a cake rack)**
**Steam basket or colander that fits into wok**
  **with rack and lid in place**

Cover rice with cold water to 2 to 3 inches
above rice. Soak for at least 3 hours or
overnight.

Drain rice and transfer to a colander or
steaming basket. Set aside.

Place a rack inside a wok and fill with water
to approximately 1-inch from rack. Cover
and heat water until boiling. Place the
colander or steaming basket on the rack
and cover. Steam for about 30 to 45
minutes or until rice is done. Make sure that
the wok does not dry out by adding boiling
water to maintain steam.

Transfer rice to a serving bowl.

# Jasmine Rice

*The lovely aroma of this rice will fill the kitchen and*
*have your mouth watering in no time. The banana leaf is a nice touch*
*if you happen to have one in the garden.*

**Makes about 6 cups**

**4 cups water**
**2 cups jasmine rice**
**2 tablespoons kosher salt**
**2 tablespoons light oil (like canola)**
**Banana leaf, optional**

## Boiling Rice Method

Bring water to a boil. Add rice, salt and oil and boil hard approximately 3 to 4 minutes. Reduce heat to simmer, cover pot and cook for 15 minutes. Remove from heat and let stand 10 minutes, covered.

Check rice with a fork or taste. If it is a little al denté, leave covered on stove with the heat off for 3 to 4 more minutes.

## Steaming Rice Method

If you have a rice steamer, proceed as you would to steam any rice. A banana leaf placed in the steamer will impart a wonderfully fragrant perfume.

Serve in individual bowls.

# Lup Cheong and Shrimp Fried Rice

*The shrimp and lup cheong combination gives this dish just a slightly different zip. Remember not to overcook the shrimp and remember also that the entire dish goes together in just a couple of minutes!*

**Makes about 6 cups**

4 ounces lup cheong (Chinese pork sausage), chopped coarsely

1/2 pound extra-large shrimp

1 tablespoon vegetable oil

2 teaspoons finely chopped garlic

2 teaspoons peeled and finely chopped ginger

1/2 cup minced celery

1/2 cup diced onion

1/2 cup peeled and diced carrots

3 cups cooked day-old white rice

1 tablespoon soy sauce

3 tablespoons oyster sauce

1/2 green onion, thinly sliced for garnish

Peel and devein shrimp. Set aside.

In a large wok, heat oil and add lup cheong. Stir-fry for about 1 minute and add shrimp. Cook shrimp quickly until it turns pink. Remove shrimp to cutting board and chop coarsely.

To the wok, add garlic, ginger, celery, and onion and cook for 1 minute. Stir in carrots and cook for 2 minutes. Add soy and oyster sauces and then shrimp and rice; toss quickly. Toss in green onions and serve.

# Sam Choy's Island Lup Cheong Fried Rice

*If you always wondered what to do with leftover rice,
here is the answer. Make a really big pot of rice so you have the 8 cups leftover.
It picks up the flavor so well. This is the real traditional fried rice.
Some say it is the best!*

**Makes about 4 cups**

**3 pieces lup cheong (Chinese pork sausage)**
**I tablespoon vegetable oil**
**I/4 cup diced onion**
**I/4 cup minced celery**
**I/4 cup peeled and diced carrots**
**I teaspoon finely chopped garlic**
**I teaspoon peeled and finely chopped ginger**
**I tablespoon soy sauce**
**I-I/2 tablespoons oyster sauce**
**3 cups cooked day-old white rice**

**Garnish:**
**I/4 cup thinly sliced green onion stalks**
**I/4 cup minced red and white kamaboko**

Cut lup cheong into thin diagonal slices.

In a large wok, heat oil and add lup cheong. Stir-fry for about
2 minutes on medium-high heat. Add onion, celery, carrots.
garlic, ginger, and stir-fry for 2 to 3 minutes over medium-high
heat.  Add soy and oyster sauces and then rice and toss
quickly.

Serve in a large bowl garnished with green onion and
kamaboko.

Sam Choy's Island Lup Cheong Fried Rice

# Lū'au Shrimp Pasta

*Shrimp and penne pasta are brought together
with lū'au leaves and the light, delicious flavor of coconut milk.
This dish could easily be called "Italy meets Hawai'i."*

**Makes about 3 cups**

8 extra-large shrimp (16 per pound)
2 tablespoons olive oil
1 medium onion, diced
1 tablespoon minced fresh garlic
2 cups chicken stock or low-sodium chicken broth
1 cup cooked lū'au leaves, chopped (see Note)
8 ounces cooked penne pasta (about 1 cup)
1/2 cup coconut milk
1 tablespoon grated Parmesan cheese

**Garnish:**
**Additional grated Parmesan cheese**

Peel and devein shrimp.

Heat the oil in a wok, adding shrimp and onions. Cook shrimp about 1 minute then turn and cook another minute. Add garlic, chicken stock, and lūau leaves. Cook about 2 more minutes until shrimp are almost cooked.

Add pasta, coconut milk, and cheese. Cook approximately 1 more minute, just enough to heat pasta through. Pour into bowl and top with additional Parmesan cheese.

**Note**
**Lū'au leaves need to be cooked long enough to prevent a scratchy throat from the oxalate crystals or, if lū'au leaves are not available, substitute with spinach.**

# Tropical Asian Spicy Pasta with Lobster

*Asian flavors blend and lobster cooks quickly.*
*Be ready to serve with the noodles, right from the pan.*

**Makes about 8 cups**

1 pound egg noodles
3/4 pound lobster meat
2 tablespoons Asian curry paste
2 tablespoons coconut milk
2 tablespoons fresh lime juice
2 tablespoons fish sauce
1 red bell pepper, deseeded and julienned
1 cup chopped garlic chives
1 cup bean sprouts
1 head bok choi, julienned
1 cup snow peas, ends trimmed
Salt and pepper to taste

Drop noodles into boiling water. Cook as package instructs and rinse with cold running water. Drain and mix with 1 teaspoon sesame oil. Set aside.

Cut lobster into 3/4-inch pieces.

In a hot wok, mix curry paste, coconut milk, lime juice, and fish sauce. Stir in lobster meat and cook about 1 minute. Add bell pepper, noodles, chives, sprouts, bok choi and snow peas and toss together. Steam for only about 1 minutes and then season with salt and pepper as necessary.

# Shiitake Mushroom Rice with Shredded Ono Stir-Fry and Fresh Spinach

*Using a delicate, delicious fish like ono
creates the balance between the mushroom and spinach flavors.
Add the jewel of rice, Basmati, and it's "'ono" all the way around.*

**Makes about 5 cups**

1 ono (wahoo) fillet, cut diagonally in thin strips
2 teaspoons light olive oil
1 small onion, julienned
1/2 cup rinsed and sliced fresh shiitake mushrooms
1 teaspoon minced fresh garlic
2 teaspoons peeled and minced fresh ginger
1/4 cup chicken stock or low-sodium chicken broth
2 tablespoons oyster sauce
1/2 pound washed and torn fresh spinach
Salt and pepper to taste
3 cups cooked Basmati rice

**Garnish:**
**Straw mushrooms**

Cut ono into strips and prepare vegetables. Set aside.

Heat a large wok and coat with oil. Stir-fry onion, shiitake mushrooms, garlic, and ginger for 1 minute. Add ono, and cook for 30 seconds, stirring constantly. Add chicken stock and oyster sauce. Cook for 1 minute.

Add spinach, cooking until wilted. Add salt and pepper to taste. Add cooked Basmati rice and toss. Cover for 1 minute.

To serve, garnish with straw mushrooms.

**Shiitake Mushroom Rice
with Shredded Ono Stir-Fry and Fresh Spinach**

# Tropical Asian Curry Paste

*Making curry paste takes a bit of time.*
*The results are worth it. Nothing seasons quite like it.*

**Makes about 3 cups**

2 tablespoons peeled and chopped fresh turmeric (see **Note**)
2 tablespoons peeled and chopped galangal
1/2 cup cilantro stems
1/4 cup peeled and chopped garlic
2 stalks lemon grass, white part only, chopped
1/4 cup fish sauce
1/4 cup fresh lime juice
1/2 cup peeled shallots
1/4 cup toasted Thai chilis
2-1/2 tablespoons coarse ground coriander seed
1 tablespoon toasted, coarse ground cumin seed
1 tablespoon toasted, coarse ground black peppercorn
1 tablespoon kosher salt
1 cup peanut oil (or canola oil)

Using a food processor and a sharp metal blade, purée the
turmeric, galangal, cilantro, garlic lemon grass and lime juice.
Make sure a smooth purée is achieved.

Add shallots, chilis, spices, and salt. While puréeing, drizzle in
the oil. Check for seasoning. Can store in refrigerator and will
hold at least 2 weeks.

**Note**
**Fresh turmeric can be substituted with 2 tablespoons ground turmeric.**

# Curried Chicken Noodles

▼▲▼▲▼▲▼▲▼▲▼▲▼▲▼▲▼▲▼▲▼▲▼

*A simple dish that can put Chinese take-out to shame.*
*No chopping, mixing or prep time. Take maybe a minute*
*to slice the chicken, chop the cabbage and then cook-um up.*
*The bed of fresh cabbage underneath adds a special crunch.*

**Makes about 4 cups**

**1 cup sliced skinless chicken**
**2 teaspoons oyster sauce**
**1 tablespoon sesame seed oil**
**1 tablespoon cooking oil**
**1 cup chop suey mix**
**1 teaspoon curry powder**
**4 ounces prepared dashi**
**2 cups fresh chow mein noodles**
**1 tablespoon cornstarch and**
**2 tablespoons water for thickening**

Marinate chicken with oyster sauce and
sesame oil.

Heat oil in wok, stir-fry chicken until brown.
Add chop suey mix and stir-fry for 1 minute.
Add curry powder, cook for 30 seconds.
Add dashi, stir and simmer for 1 minute.
Add noodles and heat. Stir in
cornstarch-water mixture to thicken to a
smooth consistency.

Serve over a bed of freshly shredded
cabbage.

# Sam Choy's Creamy Oriental Dressing

▼▲▼▲▼▲▼▲▼▲▼▲▼▲▼▲▼▲▼▲

*I invented this to go on a hundred different dishes.*
*It is easy and quick. What's even quicker?*
*Pick up my bottled version in the supermarket!*

**Makes 4 Cups**

**3 cups mayonnaise**
**1/2 cup soy sauce**
**3/4 cup granulated sugar**
**1/4 teaspoon white pepper**
**1-1/2 tablespoons black sesame seeds**
**1 tablespoon sesame oil**

Place all ingredients in a medium-size bowl and whisk together until well blended. If necessary, whisk in a few drops of water at a time until you get the consistency you want. Refrigerate until used.

# Wasabi Mayonnaise

▼▲▼▲▼▲▼▲▼▲▼▲▼▲▼▲▼▲

*Great with my Aloha Fried Poke Wrap.*
*The wasabi gives it the perfect kick!*

**Makes about 1/2 cup**

**1 tablespoon wasabi powder**
**2 tablespoons water**
**1/2 cup mayonnaise**
**salt and pepper to taste**

Make a paste of the wasabi powder and water. Whisk into mayonnaise until completely mixed. Season ith a pinch of salt and black pepper. Refrigerate.

# Sam Choy's Wasabi Vinaigrette

*This dressing has the light bite of wasabi
without the watering eyes of the pure paste.
The fresh orange juice is the surprise ingredient!*

**Makes 3 Cups**

**2 cups freshly squeezed orange juice**
**2 tablespoons sesame seeds**
**3 tablespoons granulated sugar**
**1/2 cup canola oil**
**3 tablespoons vinegar**
**2 tablespoons soy sauce**
**Salt to taste**
**2 tablespoons wasabi paste**

Combine ingredients and whisk together
until well blended and sugar is dissolved.
Refrigerate until used.

# Balsamic Wasabi Vinaigrette

*This is a very light wasabi dressing. Whisk it together quick and plan to make more. It goes fast once the family tastes it!*

**Makes 1 cup**

1 tablespoon wasabi paste
3/4 cup salad oil
1/4 cup balsamic vinegar
1/4 cup granulated sugar
1 teaspoon minced fresh garlic

Combine ingredients and whisk together until well blended and sugar is dissolved. Refrigerate until used.

# Teriyaki Sauce

*Everyone loves the island flavor of a good teriyaki sauce. What makes it great is the balance of garlic, ginger and pepper.*

**Makes 2 cups**

1 cup soy sauce
1/2 cup mirin (Japanese sweet rice wine)
1/2 cup water
1/4 cup brown sugar
2 teaspoons minced fresh garlic
2 teaspoons peeled and minced ginger
2 teaspoons garlic chili sauce or hot red pepper flakes

Combine all ingredients and mix until the sugar is dissolved. Refrigerate until used.

# Sweet and Sour Sauce

*Stir and stir. Don't let it burn.*
*The secret to this sweet sour is the orange marmalade.*

**Makes about 2 cups**

1 cup granulated sugar

1/2 cup tomato ketchup

1/2 cup vinegar

1/2 cup water plus 2-1/2 tablespoons water for
thickening

1/4 cup orange marmalade

2 tablespoons pineapple juice

1-1/2 teaspoons peeled and minced ginger

1 teaspoon minced garlic

1/4 teaspoon hot pepper sauce

2 tablespoons cornstarch

In a medium-size saucepan, combine all
ingredients except cornstarch and 1-1/2
tablespoons water for thickening. Stir until
sugar is dissolved.

Mix cornstarch with 2-1/2 tablespoons
water to form a paste. Bring sauce to a boil
and add cornstarch paste for thickening.
Reduce heat and simmer, stirring frequently
until thickened.

Use immediately or store in refrigerator until
used.

# Special Oriental Mayonnaise

*Making homemade mayonnaise takes time but there really isn't anything you can buy that is this good.*

**Makes about 1-1/2 cups**

**2 cloves fresh garlic, minced**
**1 tablespoon peeled and finely minced ginger**
**1/4 cup soy sauce**
**2 tablespoons rice vinegar**
**2 tablespoons brown sugar**
**3 whole star anise**
**1 egg**
**1 tablespoon sesame mustard**
**3/4 cup safflower oil**
**1/4 cup sesame oil**
**Several drops hot chili oil**

Combine the garlic, ginger, soy sauce, vinegar, brown sugar, and star anise in a small saucepan. Heat to boiling. Reduce heat and simmer, uncovered, for 10 minutes. Remove from heat and discard the star anise.

Process the egg and mustard in a food processor until blended, about 20 seconds. With the machine running, pour the safflower and sesame oil in a thin, steady stream to make a thick mayonnaise.

Add the reduced soy sauce mixture and process to combine. Season to desired hotness with chili oil. Spoon the mayonnaise into a bowl and refrigerate, covered, until ready to serve.

# Cutting It Right

Wok cooking requires foods to be cut right to cook right. And cutting usually takes more time than the actually cooking. So, here are the basics of cutting to insure great wok cooking every time.

The most common type of knives found in the home kitchen is a: bread knife, chef or French knife, table knife, and paring knife.

The bread knife has a long serrated blade. It's good for cutting soft foods, like bread or tomatoes,

The French knife has a broad blade and along sharp edge. It is excellent for cutting meats, poultry, and most vegetables, especially large or hard vegetables (like carrots).

The ordinary table knife is generally not sharp enough to be used in wok cooking.

The paring knife is a small knife but very sharp. This is used for cutting smaller and softer foods (like garlic).

No matter which knife you use, it is important to remember that you are less likely to cut yourself with a sharp knife handled correctly then a dull knife. The reason is that people tend to press harder with dull knives than sharp knives and therefore run the risk of cutting themselves.

Here are a few hints on correctly handing a knife.

1. Always pick up a knife by its handle never by the blade.

2. Hold the food you're cutting like a "claw". In other words such your fingers underneath your hand. This will feel uncomfortable at first, but you'll get used to it fairly quickly.

3. When holding food, make sure to hold it firmly so that it does not move. When cutting, the knife should be gently placed against your knuckle with fingers tucked underneath. Take along cuts away from yourself.

NEVER CUT WHEN YOUR FINGERS ARE POINTED OUTWARD.

4. Foods that are round or oddly shaped maybe cut in half to create a flat surface. This will keep them from moving around.

5. Use a chopping board rather than a countertop or plate.

Example of how to chop an onion.

To chop an onion, carefully sliced in half lengthwise. Peel away the skin and plays 1/2 the onion flat side down on a cutting board. Hold the onion firmly with fingers tucked underneath. Carefully cut the onion, holding the slices together. Turn the onion and cut across the slices, the result will be chopped pieces.

## Measures and Weights

1 pinch = 1/16 to 1/8 teaspoon

3 teaspoons = 1 tablespoon

1 tablespoon = 14.8 milliliters (American)

1 tablespoon = 15 milliliters (British)

4 tablespoons = 1/4 cup

5-1/3 tablespoons = 1/3 cup

8 tablespoons = 1/2 cup

16 tablespoons = 1 cup

2 cups = 1 pint

4 cups = 1 quart

2 pints = 1 quart

1.06 quarts = 1 liter

4 quarts = 1 gallon

1 fluid ounce = 2 tablespoons = 29.6 milliliters

8 fluid ounces = 1 cup

1 cup = 235.6 milliliters (American)

1 cup = 250 milliliters (British)

1 ounce = 28.35 grams

16 ounces = 1 pound

1 pound = 454 grams

2.2 pounds = 1 kilogram

## Volume versus Weight Measures

1 cup = 8 fluid ounces

1 cup may or may not weigh 8 ounces (227 grams) because of the different density of foods.

For example:

1 cup of popped popcorn equals 8 fluid ounces but only 1/3 ounce in weight (8 to 11 grams)

1 cup chopped onion equals 8 fluid ounces but only 5-1/2 ounces in weight (155 grams)

1 cup of water equals 8 fluid ounces and about 8.3 ounces in weight (236 grams)

1 cup of tomato paste equals 8 fluid ounces but 9.2 ounces in weight (262 grams)

133

# Substitution List

'ahi (yellowfin tuna) • use fresh blackfin or bluefin tuna

balsamic vinegar • use sherry vinegar

bamboo shoots • use bottled hearts of palm

bean curd stick (dried) • go to an Asian market or use thawed frozen firm tofu

bok choy • use napa cabbage or green cabbage

cayenne pepper • use any ground hot chili pepper

chili paste • use ground garlic cloves, red chili peppers, onions, and sugar

cilantro (Chinese parsley) • use parsley

coconut milk (thin) • use 1 cup whole milk beaten with 1 teaspoon coconut flavoring

coconut milk (thick) • use 1 cup heavy cream with one teaspoon coconut flavoring

cornstarch for thickening • use all-purpose flour up to 2 to 3 tablespoons

dashi (1 teaspoon) • use 1 teaspoon drained canned tuna (flaked)

enoki mushrooms • use julienned button mushrooms

fish sauce • use 1 part soy sauce plus four parts mashed anchovies

furikake • use ground sesame seeds and finely chopped nori seaweed sheets

garlic cloves (1) • use 1 teaspoon chopped garlic or 1/8 teaspoon garlic powder

ginger (fresh grated) • go to an Asian market (powdered ginger is not a good substitute)

hoisin sauce • use pureed plum baby food mixed with soy sauce, garlic, and chili peppers

kalikali (kalekale) • use any pink or red snapper such as 'opakapaka

konnyaku • use firm silken tofu

kosher salt • use coarse grain sea salt

lemon grass • use lemon zest

luau leaves • use spinach leaves

lup cheung (Chinese sausage) • use high fat pork sausage

mahimahi (dolphinfish) • use drum, halibut, cod, seabass, and wahoo

Maui onion • use Bermuda, Vidalia, Ewa, red, or other sweet onion

mirin • use sweet sherry or sweet vermouth

miso • use condensed chicken broth blended with a small amount of tofu

mung bean thread (long rice) • use any transparent noodle such as cellophane or try spaghetti squash strands

opah (moonfish) • use monchong, amberjack, jack crevalle, or trevally

panko • use finely ground dry bread crumbs

papaya • chrensaw melon will give similar color and texture but not the same flavor

peanuts, raw • use raw almonds or walnuts

poi • use unseasoned mashed potatoes thinned to a thick batter consistency

red chili pepper flakes • use finely chopped seeded red chili peppers

rice wine vinegar • use a slightly sweetened light-colored vinegar

sake • use very dry sherry or vermouth

sesame seeds • use finely chopped toasted almonds

shiitake mushrooms (fresh) • use rehydrated dry shiitake or other meaty-fleshed mushroom such as portobello mushroom

snow peas • use sugar snap peas

somen noodle • use vermicelli

soy sauce • use 3 parts Worcestershire sauce to 1 part water

teriyaki sauce • use mixture of soy sauce, sake or sherry, sugar, and ginger

wasabi (powdered) • use hot dry mustard

wasabi (1 tablespoon prepared) • use bottled prepared horseradish with a drop of green food coloring

watercress • use arugula

wing beans • use long beans or Chinese snow peas

# Glossary

Abalone—a marine gastropod mollusk with a large "ear-shaped" single shell. The most commonly consumed part is the large muscle which generally requires tenderizing by pounding or long cooking time.

'Ahi—Hawaiian name for yellowfin or bigeye tuna. Also called shibi in Japanese. Often served raw as sashimi.

Al dente —Italian phrase meaning to cook foods such as pasta and vegetables to the point that they still offer a slight resistance to the bite.

Balsamic vinegar—A vinegar made from a white grape juice and aged in wooden barrels for a period of years. It has a very dark color and special soft flavor that is picked up from the wood of the barrels used for aging.

Bamboo shoots—Cream colored, cone shaped young shoots of the bamboo plant. Canned shoots are fine to use.

Basil—fresh or dried herb available in a variety of types including common sweet basil, opal basil, and Thai basil. These varieties can be used interchangeably.

Bean curd sticks—A dried soybean product that is softened by soaking before use. It is commonly used in place of meat in mixed dishes.

Bean sprouts—Usually refers to sprouted mung beans, however soy beans, lentils, and sometimes other beans are used in sprouted form. Generally consumed raw or lightly stir-fried.

Bean thread noodles—A thin, clear noodle made from the starch of the mung bean. These relatively flavorless noodles soak up the flavors of other ingredients in a dish. Also called cellophane noodles.

Bok choi or bok choy—also known as pak choy or Chinese white cabbage. It has dark green leaves and long white stems.

Bonito Flakes—dried tuna shavings.

Chili oil—vegetable oil flavored with hot chilies by steeping them in the oil. Should be kept in the refrigerated.

136

Chili paste—the composition of pastes vary, but generally include hot red chilies, vinegar, salt, and possibly garlic.

Chili sauce—these sauces, composed of chili peppers, vinegar, salt, and sugar, range from sweet and mild to very hot.

Chow mein noodles—Chinese noodles generally made from wheat flour and eggs, sold dried or fresh.

Cilantro—leaves of the coriander plant. Also known as Chinese parsley.

Coconut milk—the liquid extracted by squeezing the grated meat of a coconut.

Dashi—Japanese word for a basic soup stock made from vegetables and dried fish (bonito tuna) flakes, and kombu (kelp) and water.

Dice—a cut into a 1/4-inch to 1/2-inch cube.

Dijon mustard—mild to hot prepared mustard originally from Dijon, France.

Dungeness crab—a large, meaty crab that ranges from one to four pounds per crab and can be purchased fresh, frozen, or canned.

Enoki mushroom —very small mushroom with spaghetti-like strands; crunchy in texture.

Fermented black beans—know as Chinese black beans or salty black beans.

Fish sauce—a concentrated salty, brown liquid, typically made from anchovies fermented in brine.

Furikake—a seasoning made from dried seaweed, sesame seeds, and salt that is used to add flavor and color to rice and noodles.

Ginger—root of a variety of ginger that is used as a seasoning both in savory dishes (typically with garlic and soy sauce).

Hawaiian chili pepper—a very small (1/2 to 1-inch long) and extremely hot pepper; substitute with red jalapeños or red serranos.

Hoisin sauce—a thick reddish-brown fermented sweet soy bean sauce that is seasoned with garlic and chile peppers.

Japanese eggplant—this purple or green smooth-skinned fruit is long (6 to 12-inches) and thin (about 1 to 2-inches diameter) and is also known as the Asian eggplant.

Julienne—to cut into matchstick-size pieces.

Kaffir lime leaf—the fibrous leaf of the kaffir lime used to impart a citrus flavor and aroma to many cooked dishes; sometimes substituted for lemon grass.

Kali kali—commonly used today to mean opakapaka, however in ancient times, kale-kale was used to represent the most mature stage of the fish.

kosher salt—coarse mild salt.

Lemon grass—Key ingredient in Thai cooking that adds a lemon flavor and fragrance to soups and other dishes. Since the grass is very fibrous, it is not consumed unless ground into a fine powder. Sometimes substituted for kaffir lime leaves.

Long Rice—Translucent thread-like noodles made from mung bean flour. Typically they are soaked in water before cooking.

Lop Cheong—Chinese pork sausage.

Lūʻau leaf—young taro leaves; cook thoroughly 50-60 minutes before eating; used in laulau; has come to mean a "feast" where laulau is traditionally served.

Macadamia Nuts—A rich flavorful nut that is a major crop in Hawaiʻi. The nut is very high in fat. So, consume in moderation and store refrigerated or frozen to prevent rancidity of the oils.

Mahimahi—also called dolphinfish, but not related to the marine mammal. Any firm-fleshed fish can be substituted in recipes.

Maui onions—large white onion noted for its sweet flavor, grown in Kula, the up country region of Maui. Substitute with other sweet onions, such as Vidalia or Ewa onions.

Mince—a fine dice, 1/8-inch cubes.

Mirin—Japanese sweet rice wine used to add sweetness and flavor to many Japanese dishes. If mirin is unavailable, use 1 tablespoon cream sherry or 1 teaspoon sugar for each tablespoon mirin.

Miso—Japanese word for fermented soybean paste; miso is often used as the base for a broth. There are several varieties that range in color from white to dark brown, with the darker misos more strongly flavored.

Mussels—imported to Hawai'i from New Zealand, are sold in local supermarkets frozen, previously frozen, or canned.

Ono is also called wahoo—A member of the mackerel family, often used for sashimi. Grouper, snapper, or sea bass can be substituted.

Opah is also called moon fish—Has pinkish flesh. Substitute with swordfish or tuna.

'Opakapaka—Hawaiian pink snapper. Substitute with red snapper or grouper.

Oyster Sauce—A concentrated dark-brown sauce made from oysters, salt, and soy sauce. Used in many Asian dishes to impart a full, rich flavor. Also available in vegetarian forms.

Panko—Japanese coarse bread crumbs used for Crunchy deep-fried coatings.

Papaya—in Hawai'i this sweet, yellow, pear-shaped fruit is about 6 to 10-inches long. A common size would yield about 1-1/2 to 2 cups flesh.

Poke—Hawaiian word for "slice"; refers to a traditional Hawaiian dish of sliced raw seafood, fresh seaweed, Hawaiian salt, and Hawaiian red chili peppers.

Portuguese sausage—pork sausage with spicing that ranges from mild to hot. Italian sausage can be substituted if necessary.

Prawns—term loosely used to describe any large shrimp, especially those less than 15 per pound.

Rice Ribbon Noodles—A flat rice noodle commonly used in Thai cooking.

Rice Wine—Typically made from steamed glutinous rice, this type of wine is found as various types in Japan such as sake and mirin and in China as chia fan, and yen hung.

Sambal oelek—fiery-hot chili paste. A table condiment in Indonesia.

Sesame Oil—Oil pressed from the sesame seed is available in two forms. Pressing the raw seed produces an oil which is light in color and flavor and can be used for a wide variety of purposes. When the oil is pressed from the toasted sesame seed, it is dark in color with a much stronger flavor.

Shiitake mushrooms—Japanese name for a black- to buff-colored mushroom used both fresh and dried. The texture is meaty and the flavor is full. Dried shiitake need to be soaked until soft (20 to 30 minutes). Also called black Chinese mushrooms and forest mushrooms.

shoyu—see SOY SAUCE

Snow peas—young edible-podded sugar peas consumed when the pods are thin and the seeds are still tiny.

Soy sauce—Commonly known as shoyu in Hawai'i, soy sauce is a salty liquid made from fermented boiled soybeans, roasted barley or wheat , monosodium glutamate (MSG), and salt. Usually dark brown in color, it is the principal seasoning in many styles of Asian cooking.

Teriyaki—Japanese word for a marinade or sauce for meat or fish; generally consisting of soy sauce, sugar, ginger, and garlic.

Thai basil—See basil.

Thai Noodles—See Rice Ribbon Noodles.

Tofu—Japanese name for a bland-flavored soy bean curd that can be custard-like in texture (soft tofu) or quite firm. The firm or extra firm forms are generally used in stir-frying or deep-frying.

Wasabi—also called Japanese horseradish; comes in both powder and paste forms and is frequently dyed bright green.

Watercress—a member of the mustard family with crisp dark green leaves that have a slightly bitter and peppery taste.

# Index

# Notes

# Notes

# Notes